Drawing book

Mastering Zendoodle Flowers and Butterflies

By Irene Blount

Table of Contents

Disclaimer

While all attempts have been made to verify the information provided in this book, the author does assume any responsibility for errors, omissions, or contrary interpretations of the subject matter contained within. The information provided in this book is for educational and entertainment purposes only. The reader is responsible for his or her own actions and the author does not accept any responsibilities for any liabilities or damages, real or perceived, resulting from the use of this information.

The trademarks that are used are without any consent, and the publication of the trademark is without permission or backing by the trademark owner. All trademarks and brands within this book are for clarifying purposes only and are the owned by the owners themselves, not affiliated with this document.

Introduction

Butterflies are a standout amongst the loveliest creatures nature has delivered. It truly is normally a fantastic experience at whatever point you watch a butterfly humming near you. They look truly peaceful An artist would normally wish to sketch among these lovely creatures when has inside the serene environment of your lawn. A butterfly sketch may be anything but difficult to make in the event that you need to try it out.

How you can sketch a butterfly?

You can sketch a butterfly in various strategies. It is subject to what kind of butterfly you might want to sketch. Its normally fantastic to begin having a clear butterfly sketch. You can draw preparatory sketches with simple diagrams. Pick unmistakable postures of the butterfly. You must be to a great degree wary while sketching butterfly wings that are basically the most key a portion of ones sketch. Initially you must envision on the off chance that you need the wings broad spread or covered. On the off chance that you like covered wings then give close center to which way you require them to cover.

At the point when you've got your layouts all set then you can go as to the enumerating segment of it. You have to continue preparing the layout sketch to have it right. The layout with the whole sketch holds the key so in the occasion you need to acquire the sketch appropriate get the diagram perfect. The most ideal path for you actually to start is by mastering the clear plans introductory after which exchanging on to the unpredictable ones.

Sorts of butterfly sketch

Butterflies are such shocking creatures that they look incredible in any sketch. They end up being regular subjects in lawn scenes botanical by and by lives and improving paintings. There are numerous systems through which you can make a butterfly sketch, for example, pencil sketch graffiti sketch tattoo sketch and toon sketch.

Precisely where is it conceivable to utilize butterfly sketches?

Butterflies look absolutely shocking in any medium of painting. They are getting to a great degree well known in craftsmanship displays wallpapers print and realistic media etc. Butterfly sketches are unimaginably far reaching in tattoos. Women worship to get butterflies tattooed on their body since it not just appears to be lovely all things considered it can make them encounter more dynamic and colorful much the very same way like a butterfly.

Butterflies are as often as possible used in enriching items like inside decorations bone china centerpieces sheets and window ornaments. The butterfly sketch contrasts in relying upon the medium colors and composition utilized.

Chapter 1 – How to draw butterfly

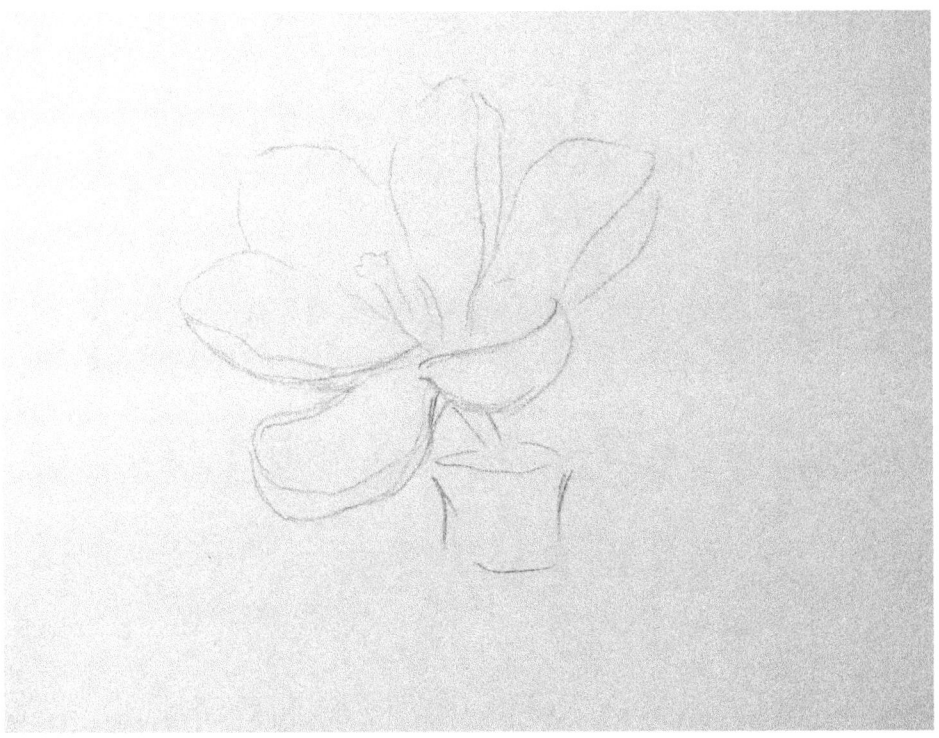

Step 1: In this initial step you will be drawing out the fundamental edge of a butterfly. To start with begin by drawing four even lines for the top, upper mid area, center, and base.

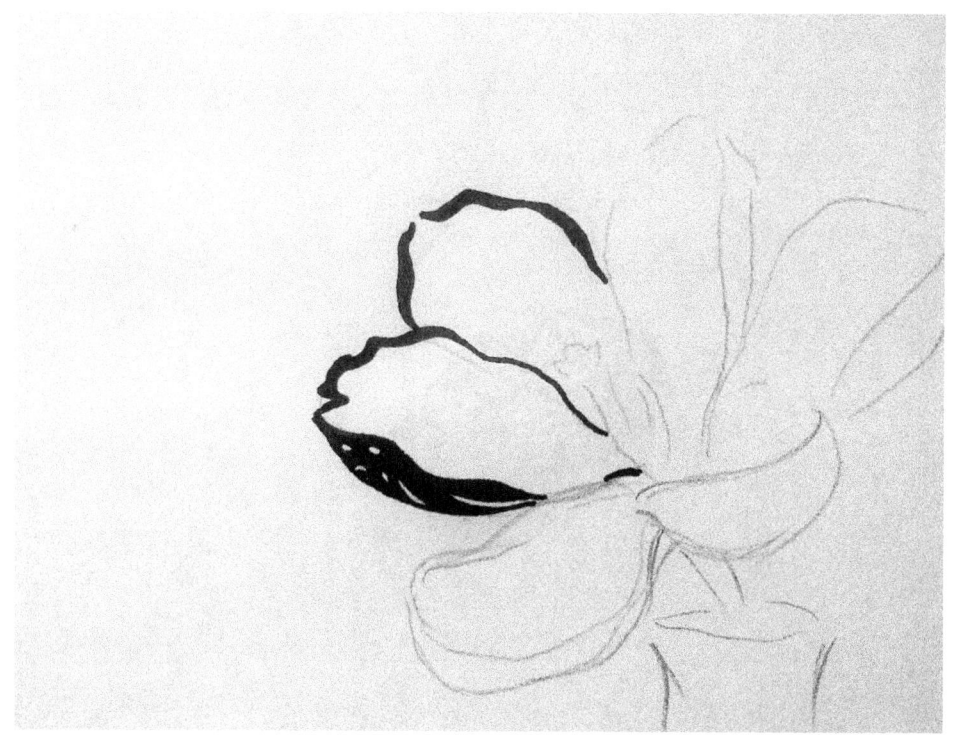

Step 2: Next draw two vertical lines to offer you some assistance with keeping the sides of the lower wings uniform. Presently draw the diagram of the wings utilizing the rules to help you. Presently you can draw parts of the butterfly's inward body like the end part which is truly the stomach on the off chance that you recollect from the depiction piece of the instructional exercise.

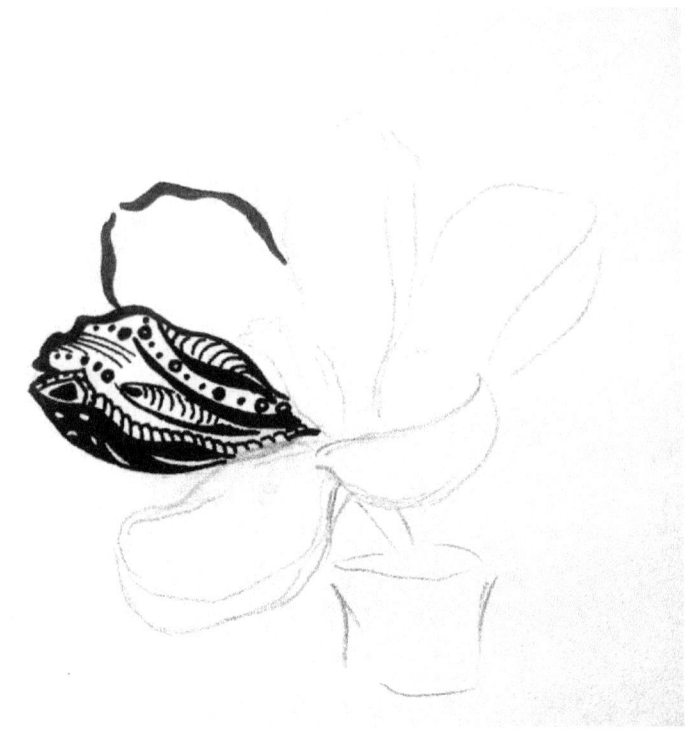

Step 3: Presently this stride ought to be short and easy to finish. You should simply plot the edge of the wings to give them a decent swell look to give the fantasy of authenticity.

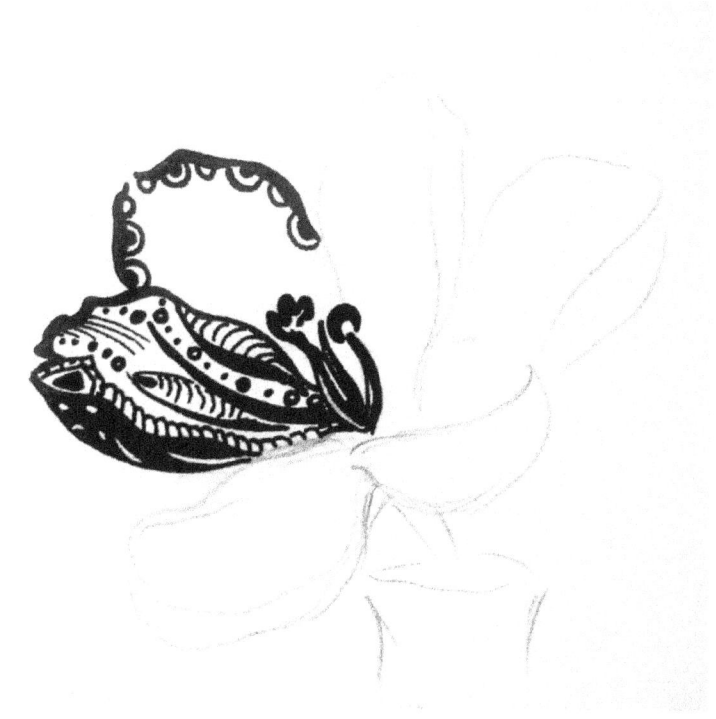

Step 4: Presently what you do after you sketch that out is softly sketch within the body of the butterfly by drawing the external edge.

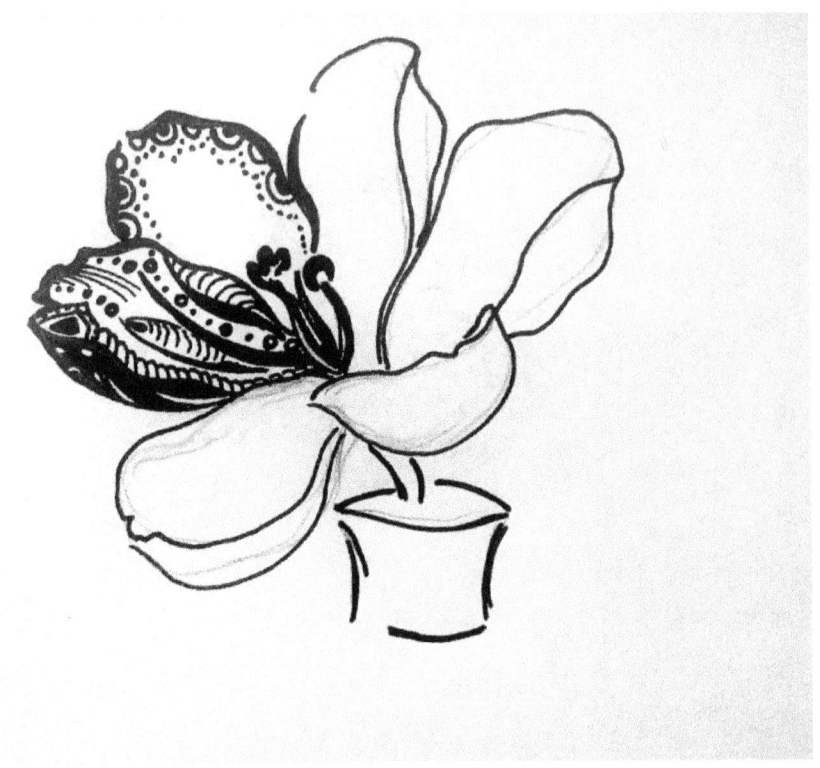

Step 5: Presently in this stride you will invest the most energy sketching and drawing out the whole example of the imprints over the wings. This will take you a few minutes to finish.

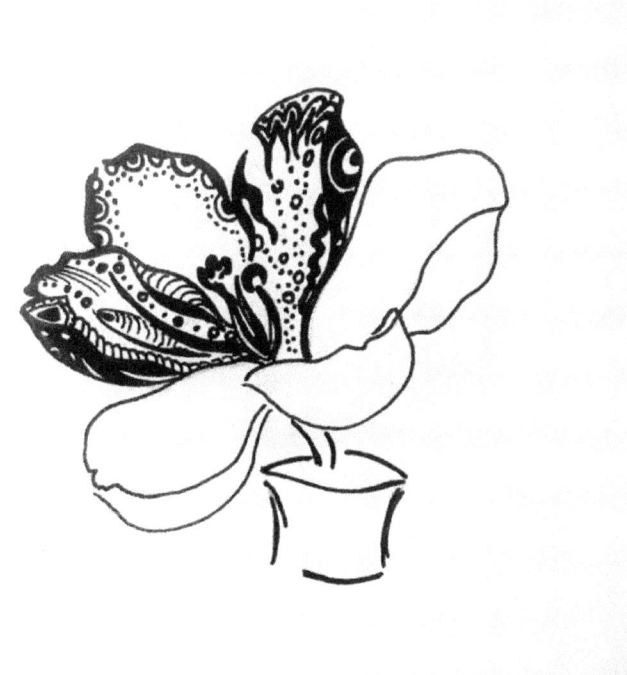

Step 6: How you need to begin this stride is by drawing the greater examples first then draw out the little ones until you come to the finishes of the wings and they simply transform into circle shapes. After you at last complete that you can simply ahead and delete every one of the rules and sketch checks and move to the following step.

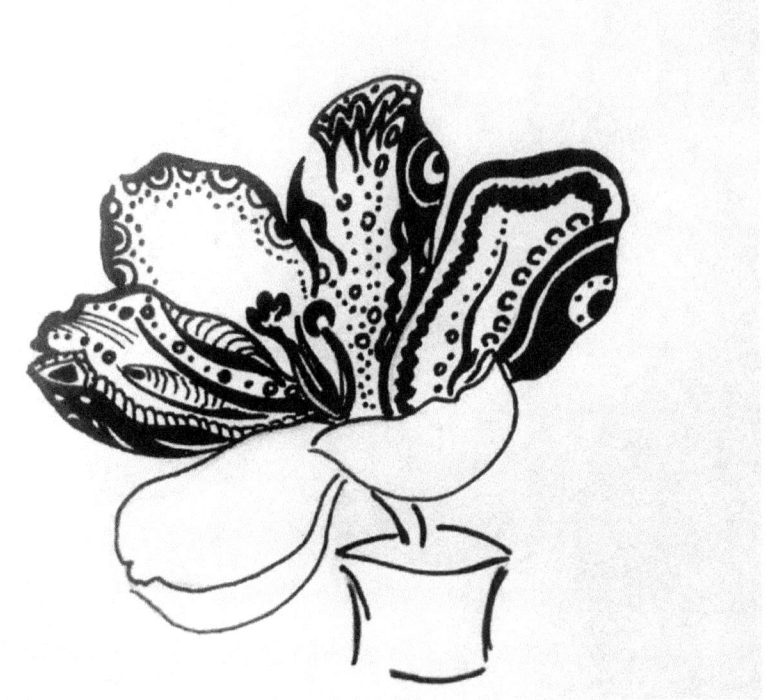

Step 7: Here is the last step, which is the completed sketch. All that is left to do is utilize your imagination and color the ruler butterfly in. After all you set aside an ideal opportunity to draw it out now joys yourself by coloring him in. See you next time kindred artist.

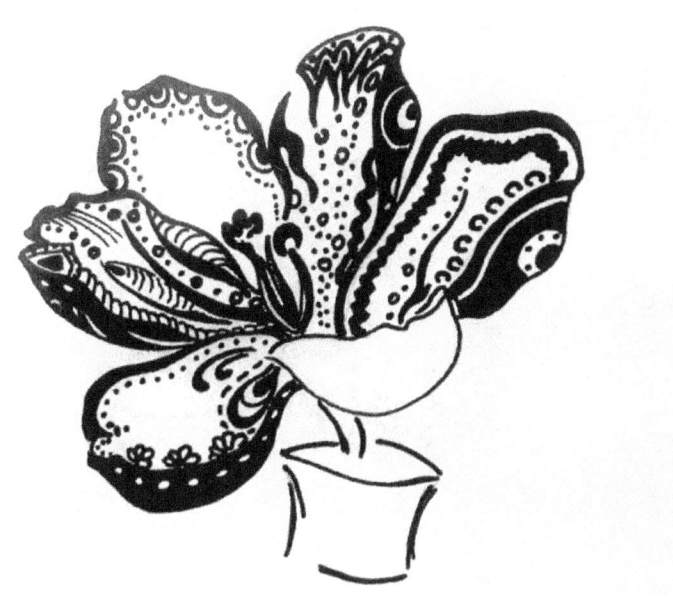

Step 8: You will now draw the wavy looking reception apparatuses and afterward sketch out the state of the butterfly's head in more detail.

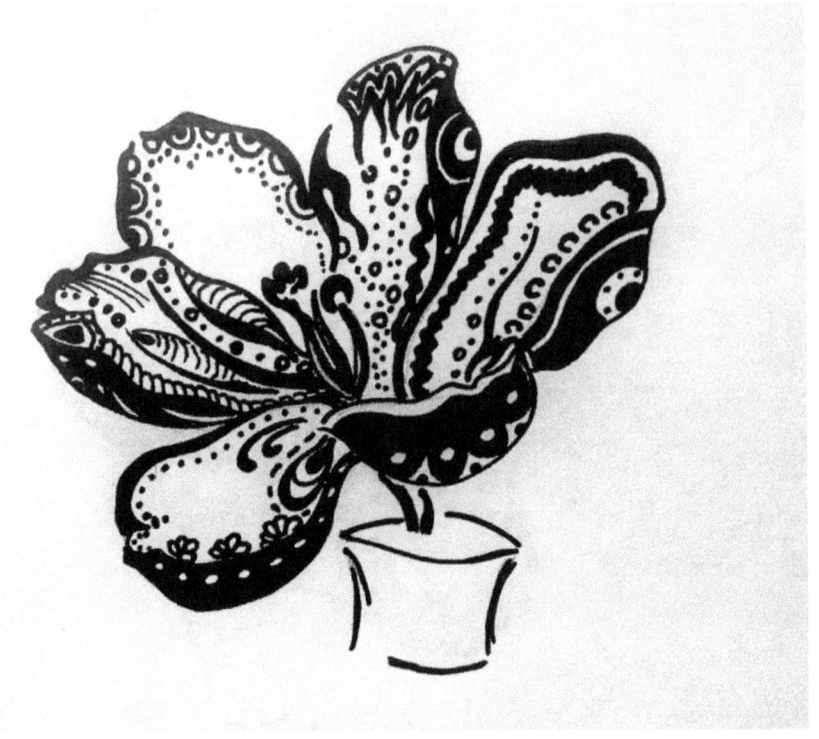

Step 9: Next begin sketching out the body of this creepy crawly.

Step 10: Draw the whole state of the body and after that draw the circle for the eye and in addition a few vertical lines on the body as you see here.

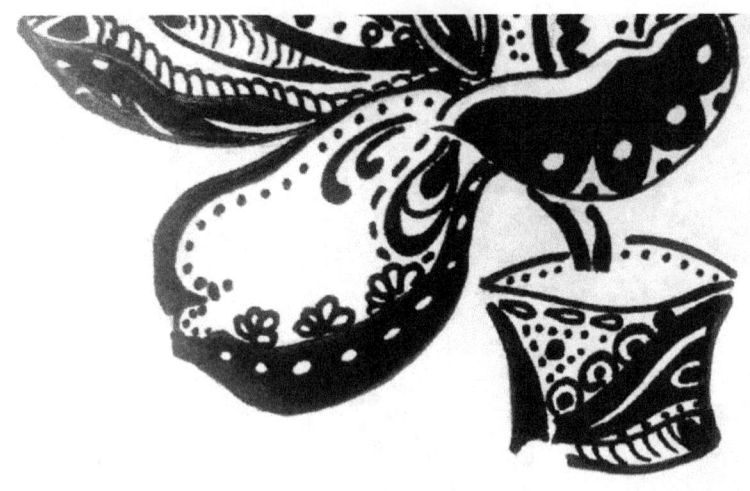

Step 11: At the point when that is done sketch out the shape and style of your butterfly wings and after that include some lovely outline markings as you see here.

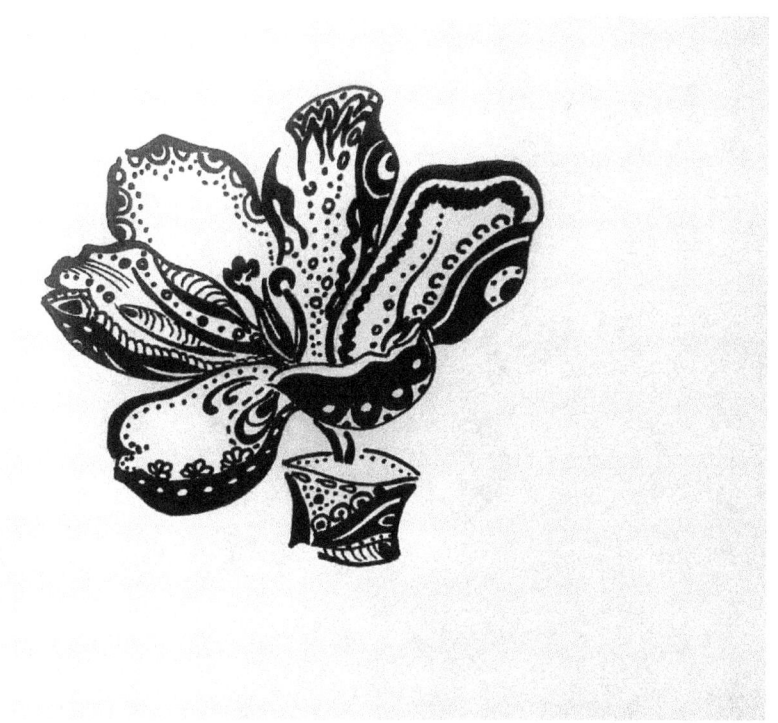

Step 12: You have made it to your last drawing step. Everything you need to do now is sketch in whatever is left of the wing outline and after that eradicate the unmistakable rules and shapes that you attracted step one.

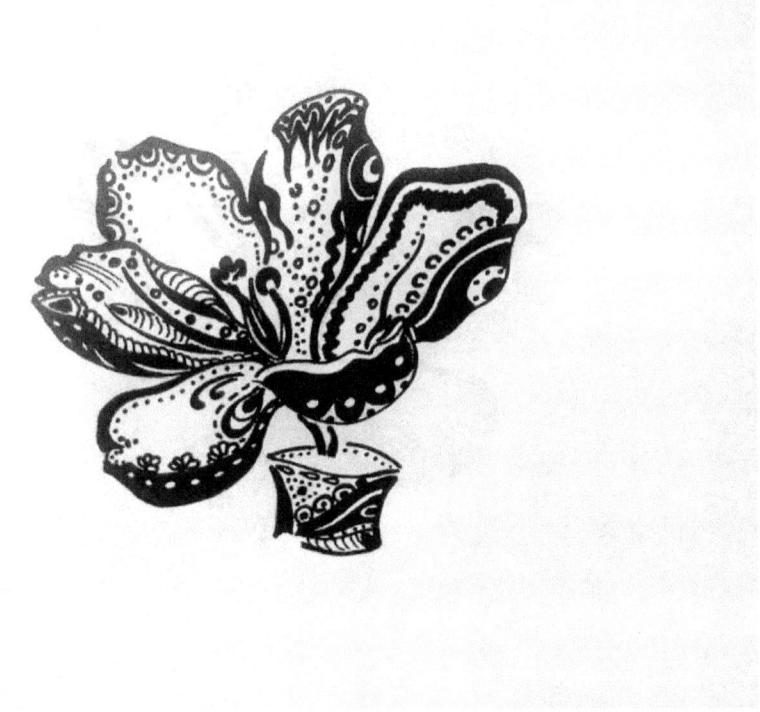

Step 13: Now you can sketch the parts which are necessary.

Chapter 2 – How to draw a butterfly

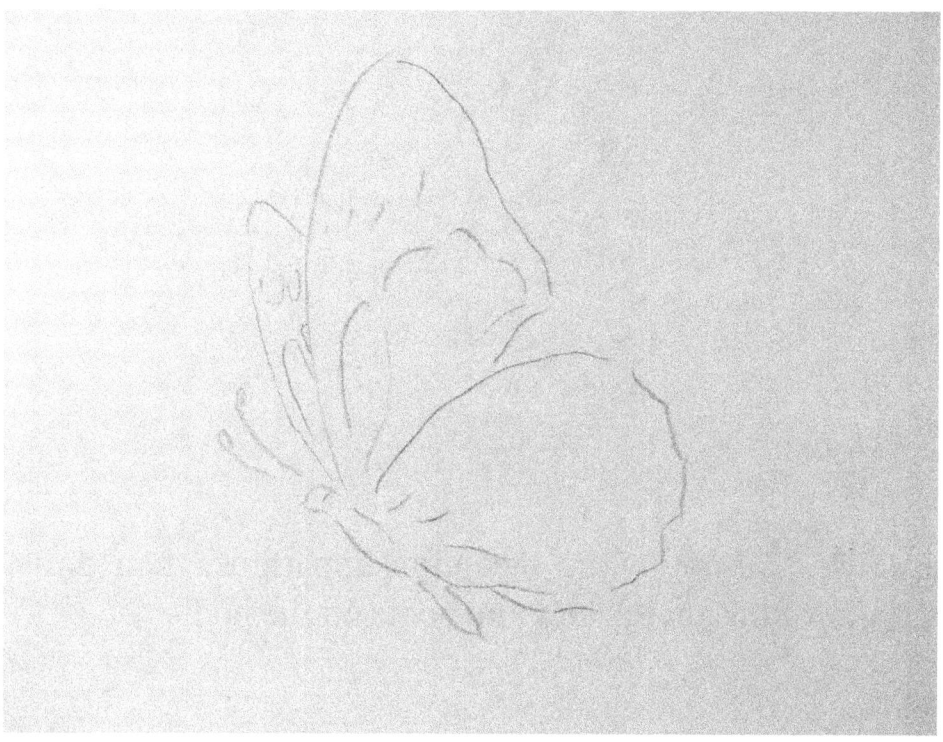

Step 1: Begin your initial step by making a little hover for the leader of the butterfly, then draw out the long diseased looking body.

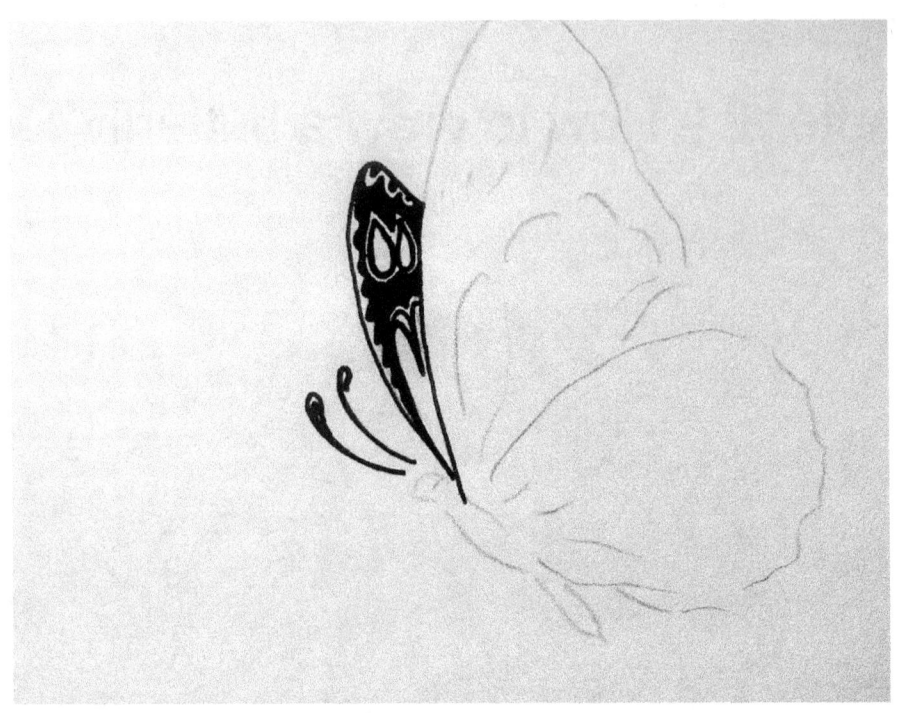

Step 2: Next, draw in the reception apparatus, then draw the eyes, and in addition the legs and spots on the body.

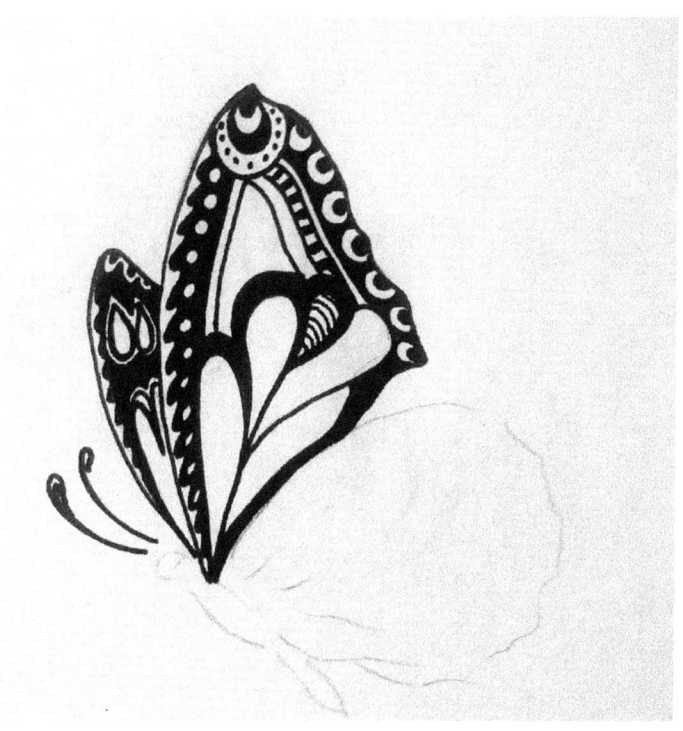

Step 3: Since the butterfly is being drawn from the side you should simply draw out the butterfly wing configuration.

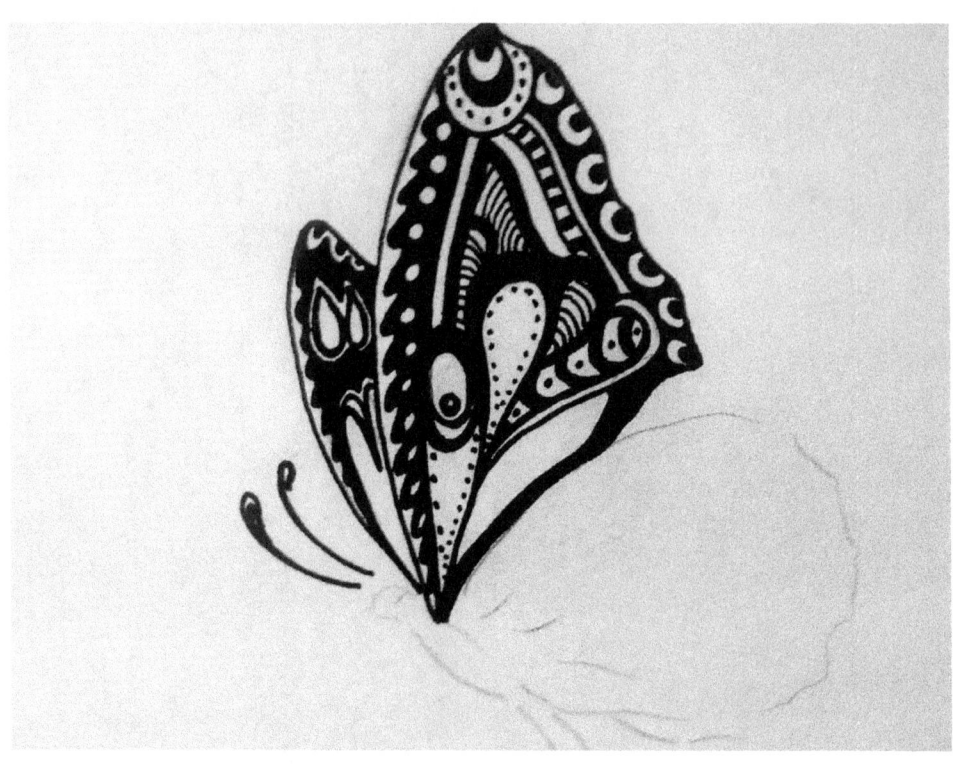

Step 4: Pick the sort if style you need for the wings.

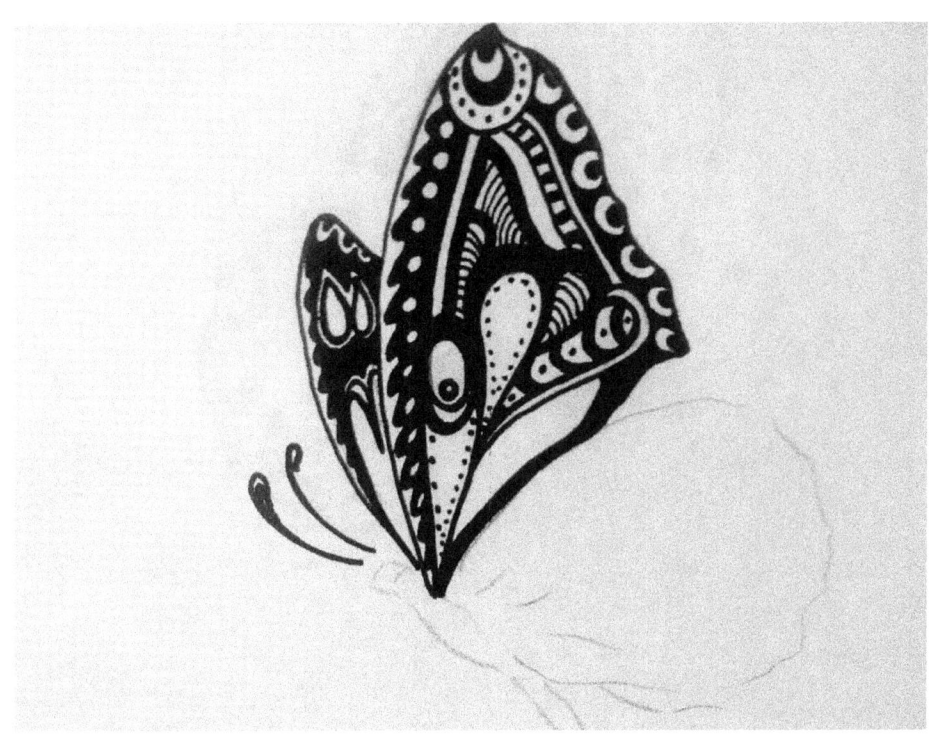

Step 5: sketch in the configuration design on the wings, then you can include more changes in the event that you like.

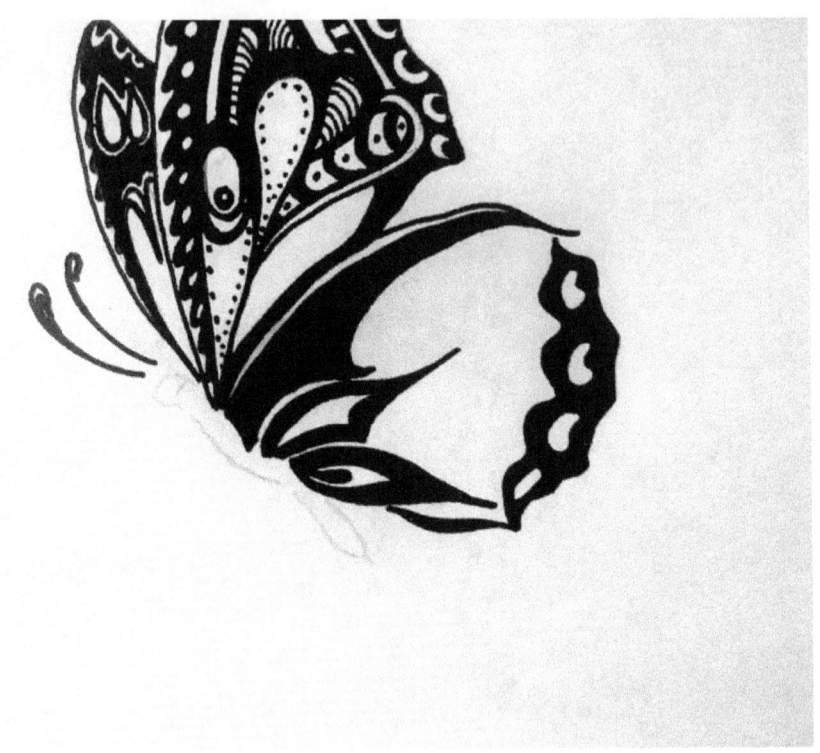

Step 6: Keep on drawing so as to deal with the butterfly out whatever is left of the example on the wings which likewise happen to be the little super thin veins.

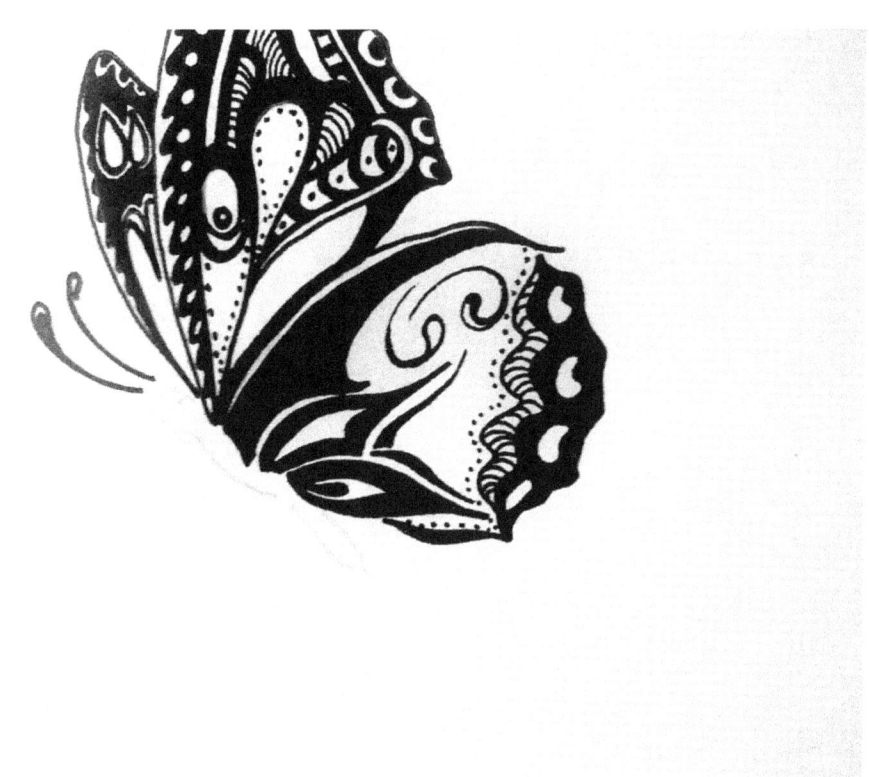

Step 7: Draw the eyes of the butterfly.

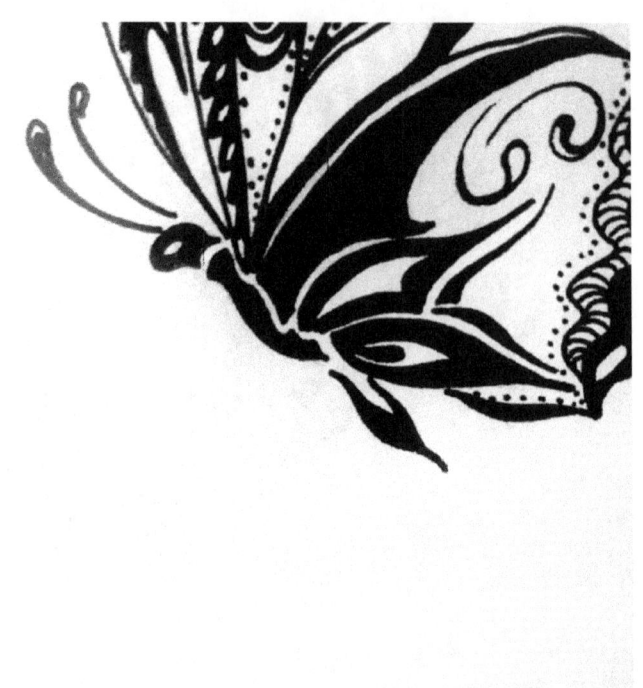

Step 8: You can run with a bloom, yet I ran with one formed like a poinsettia.

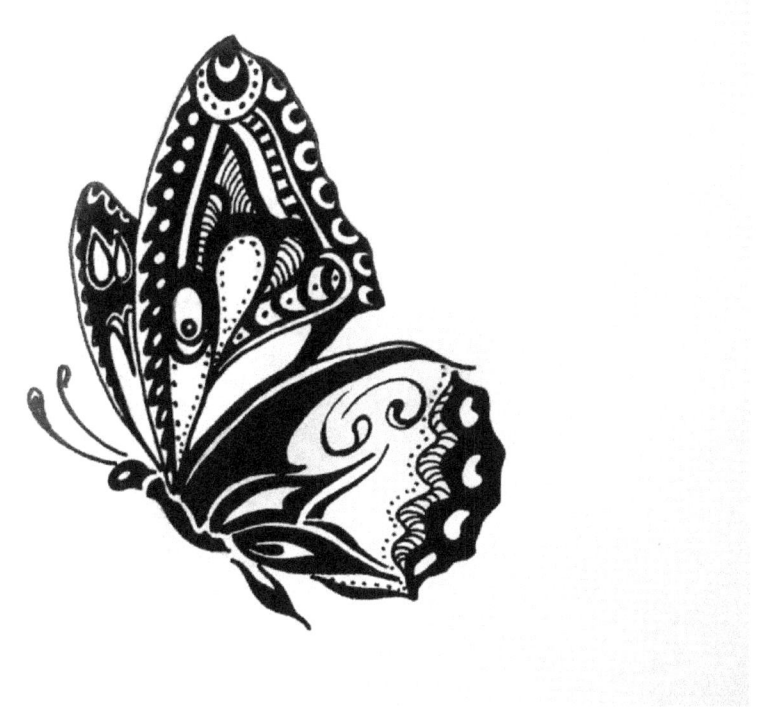

Step 9: Add itemizing to each unmistakable petal before you begin tidying up the drawing liberating it from errors.

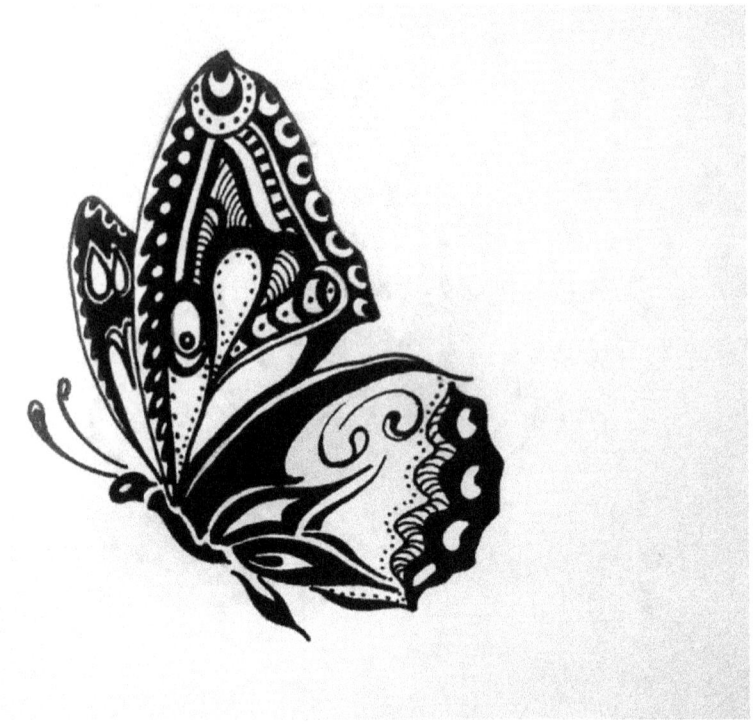

Step 10: Here is the thing that the butterfly looks like when you are finished. Color it in and that is it. Wasn't that a fun drawing to make? Presently you can indicate people what you have done.

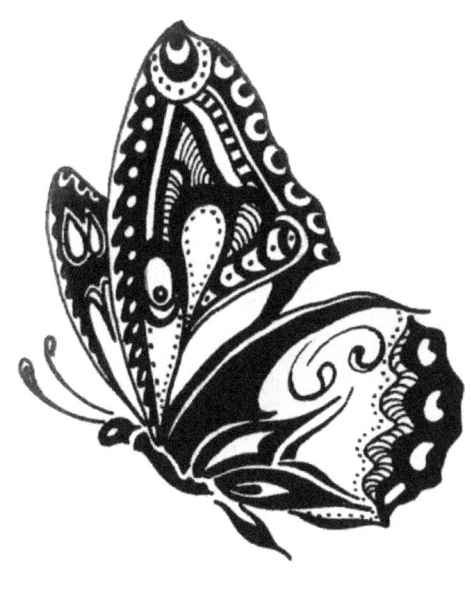

Step 11: Now you can sketch the parts which are necessary.

Chapter 3 – How to draw butterfly

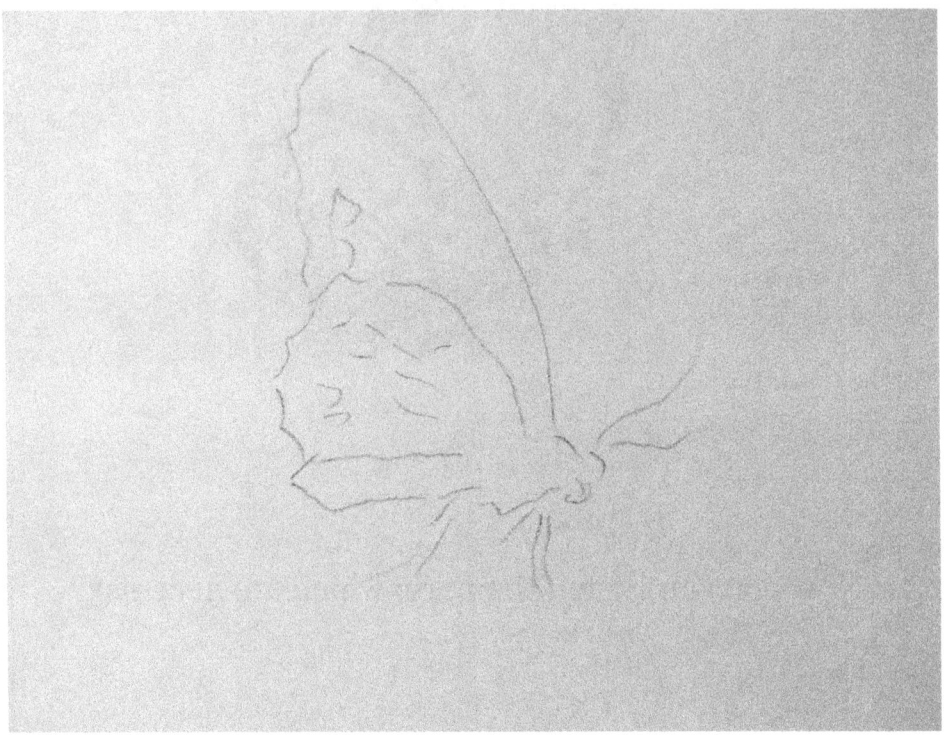

Step 1: Begin by drawing an oval shape for the butterfly's body, and after that draw a lower level line like you see here.

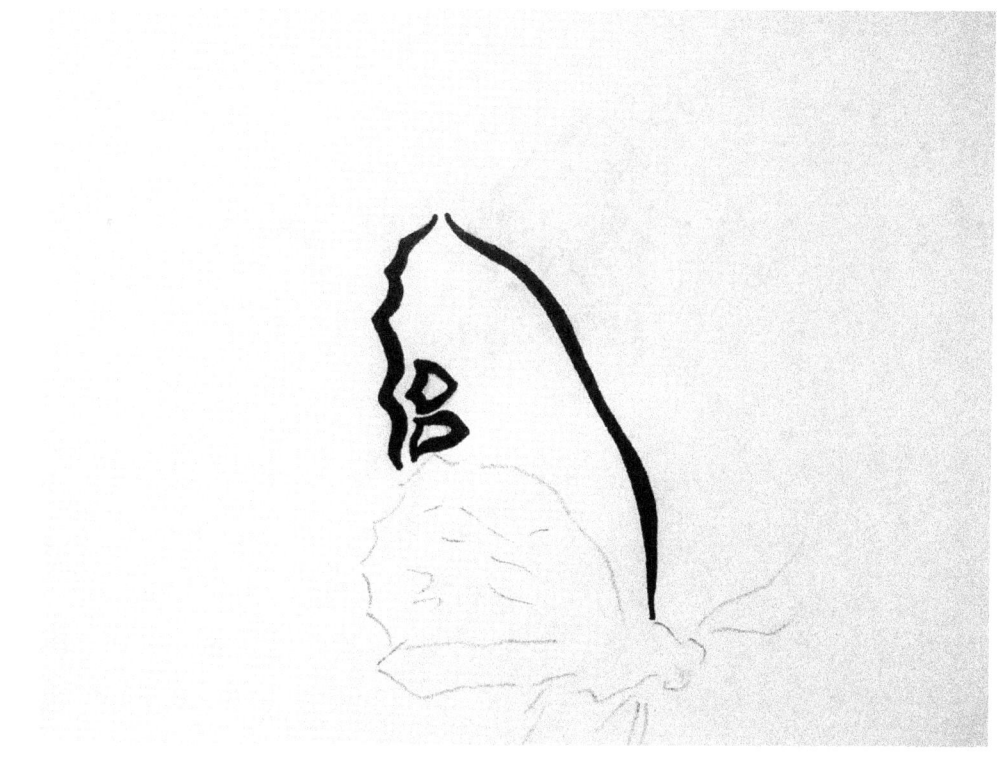

Step 2: Presently you should simply utilize the level line you attracted step one as a manual for make your wings even and aliened with one another.

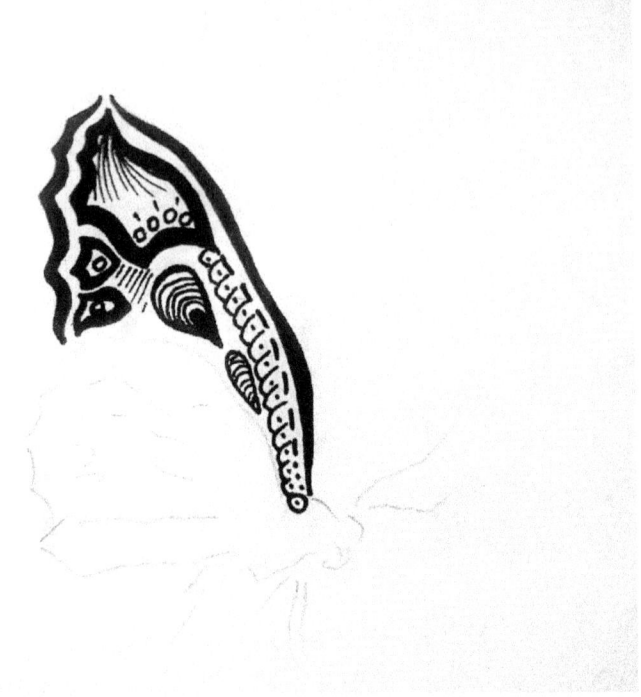

Step 3: What you will do now is draw out the body a bit skinnier then you initially attracted step one. In the meantime, consolidate the butterfly's radio wires with the coating configuration you are doing now.

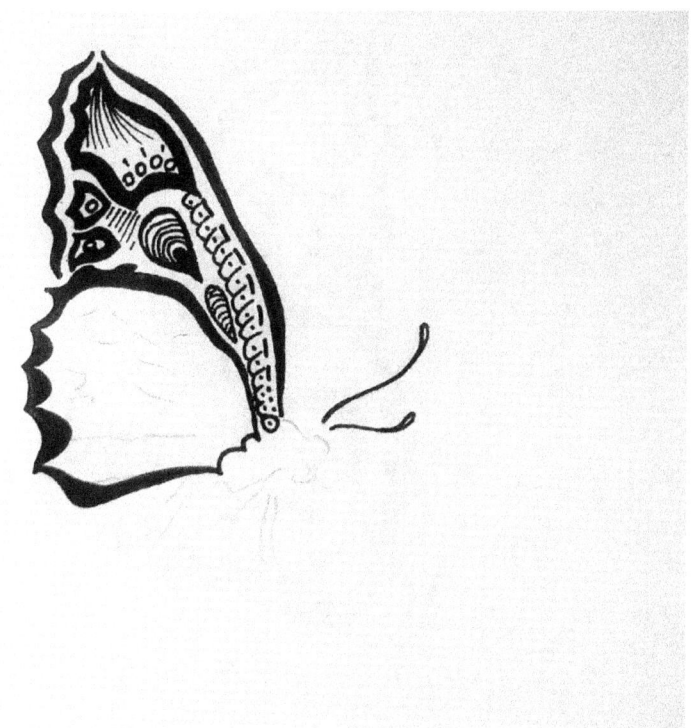

Step 4: For your last drawing step, you should simply draw in the level lines on the body, and after that include the different recognizes the wings if that is the sort of outline example you like. Eradicate the lines and shapes that you attracted step one to set up your butterfly for color.

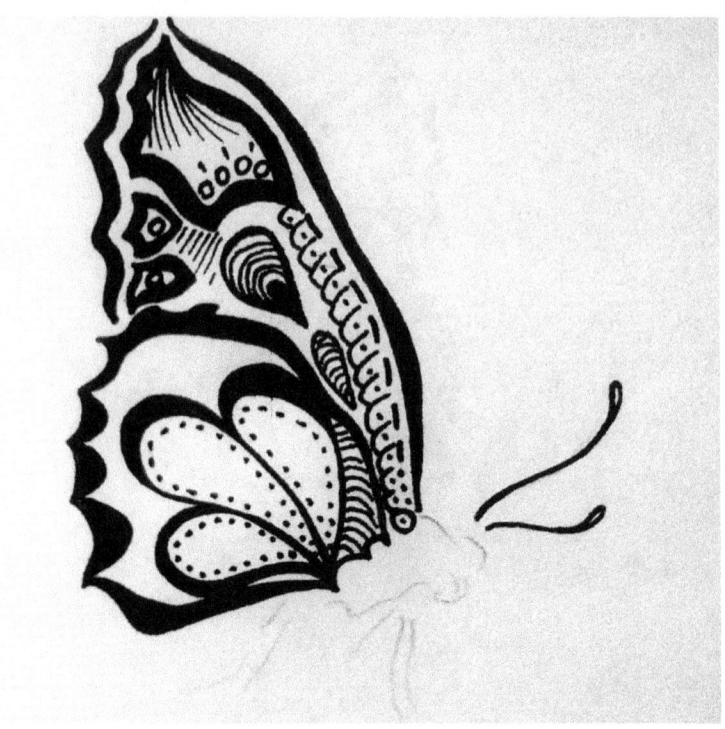

Step 5: Here is the way your butterfly looks when you are all done. Presently you can color it in whatever you like. I trust you enjoyed this lesson on drawing a simple butterfly.

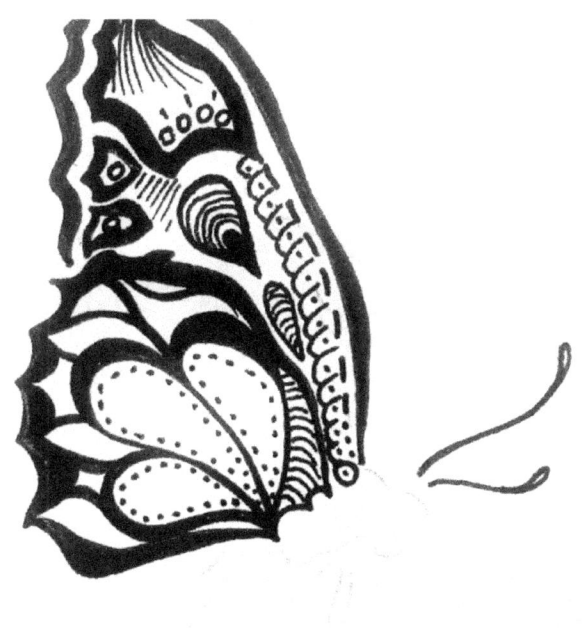

Step 6: OK, the title says it all; this will be an exceptionally straightforward drawing instructional exercise that will show you to draw a butterfly, effectively. Begin with a little hover for the leader of the creepy crawly. Draw a straight vertical line from the head for the body, and afterward draw two semi angled lines which will be for the highest point of the wings.

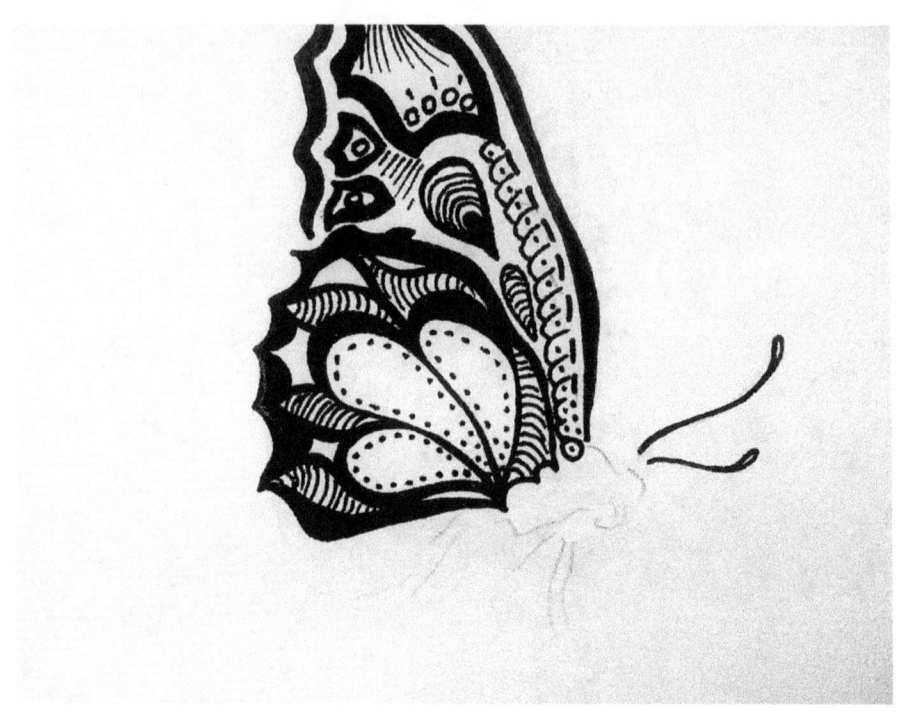

Step 7: What you will do here is draw out the illustrated picture of a butterfly like you see here. This incorporates the wings, head, and body.

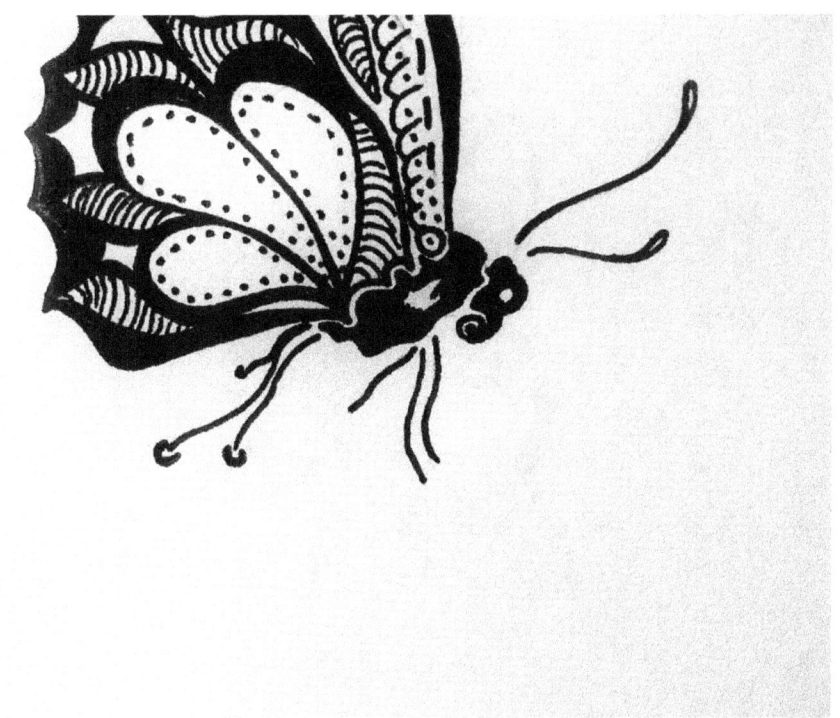

Step 8: Next, draw precisely the same shape inside of the butterfly wings. This will give you the outskirt or confining that the wings are laid out with. At the point when that is done, draw two wavy reception apparatus. Keep in mind; this is a straightforward adaptation of a butterfly.

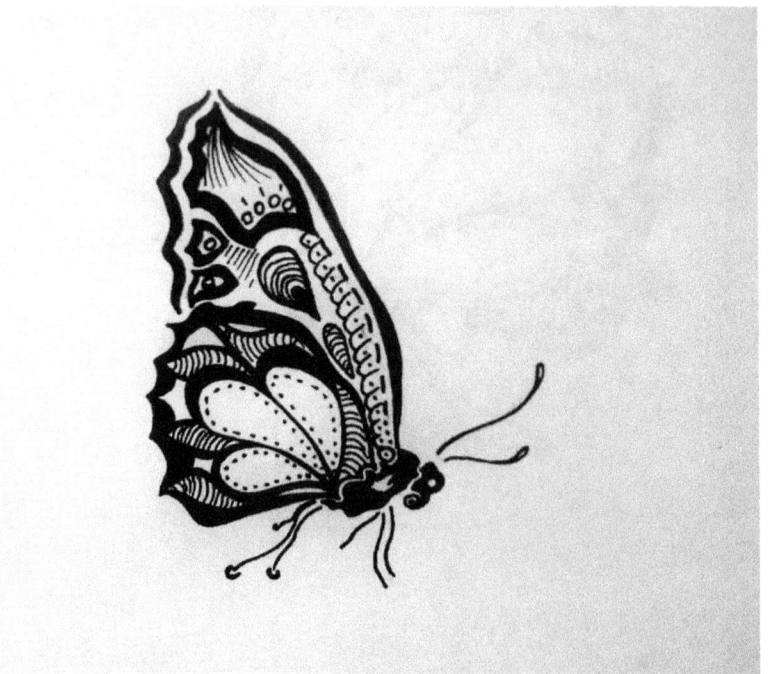

Step 9: For your last drawing step, you should simply draw in some outline designs on the wings. You can play with the stamping shapes, and their sizes.

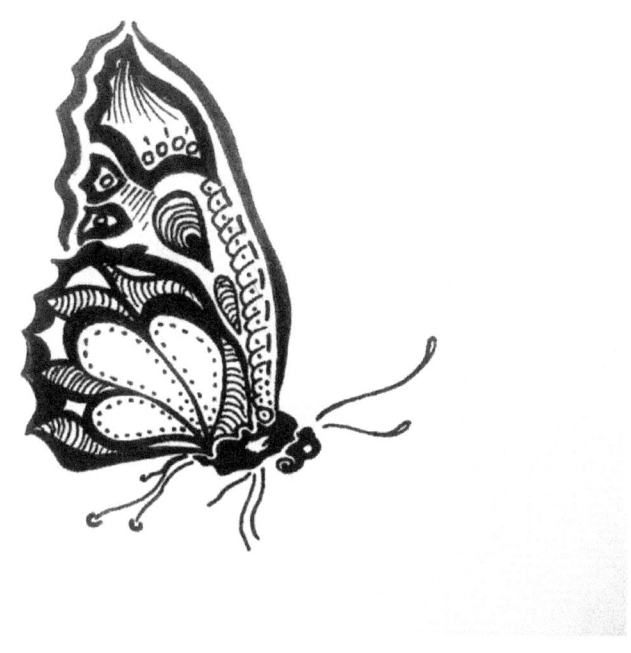

Step 10: At the point when all is said and done your butterfly ought to turn out looking like the one you see here.

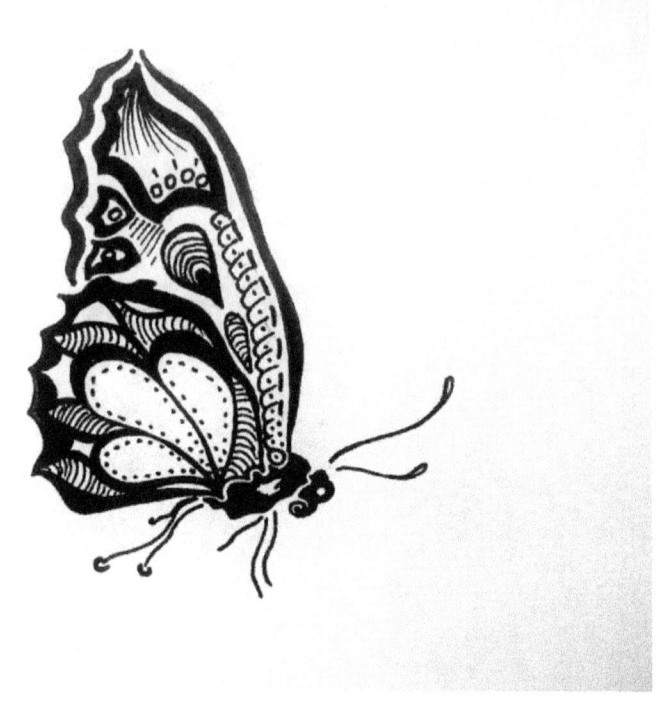

Step 11: Now you can sketch the parts which are necessary.

Chapter 4 – How to draw a flower

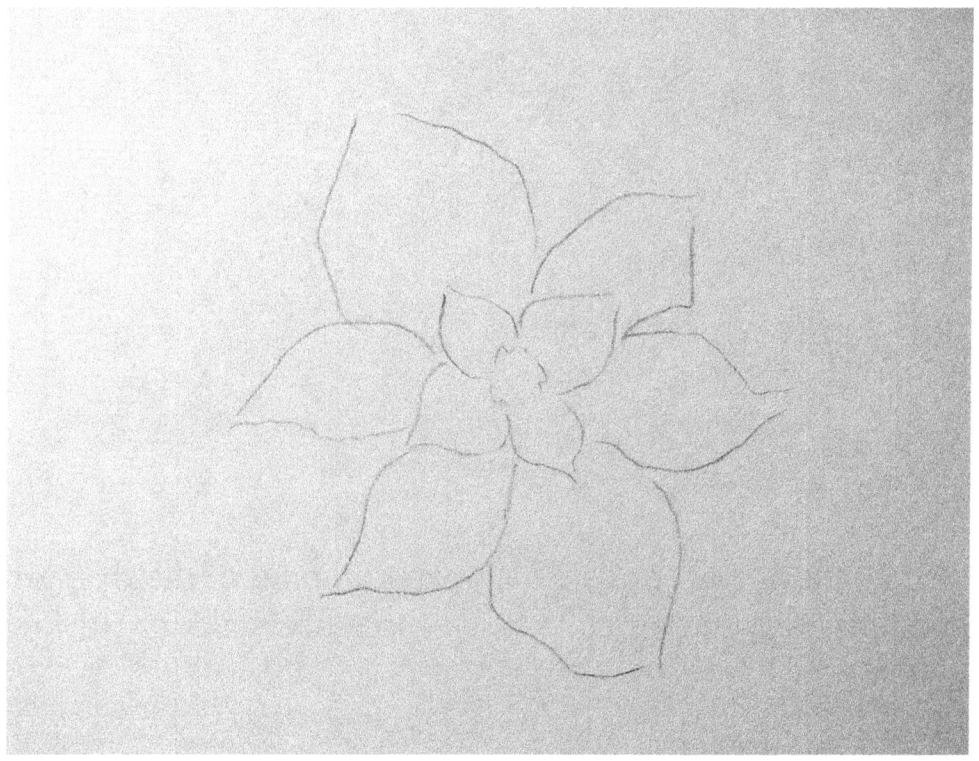

Step 1: Give us a chance to begin with the development of a sprout which is likewise called the focal point of the rose.

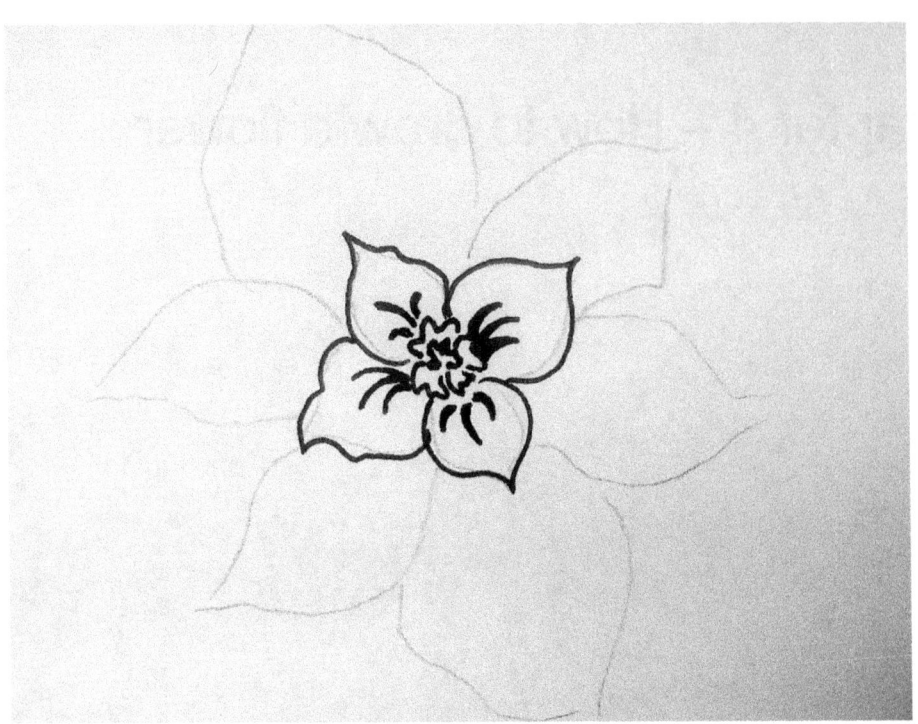

Step 2: Up next, start drawing a greater amount of the rose petals like in this way, there ought to be three areas taking all things together.

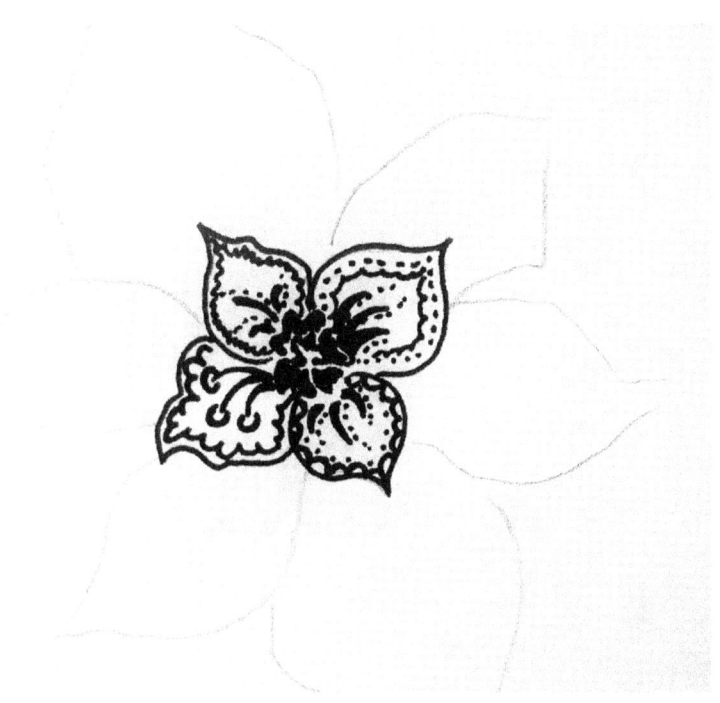

Step 3: We will proceed with adding so as to draw the rose more petals. This time draw them in layers. This will frame a full rose blossom when you are finished with every one of the strides.

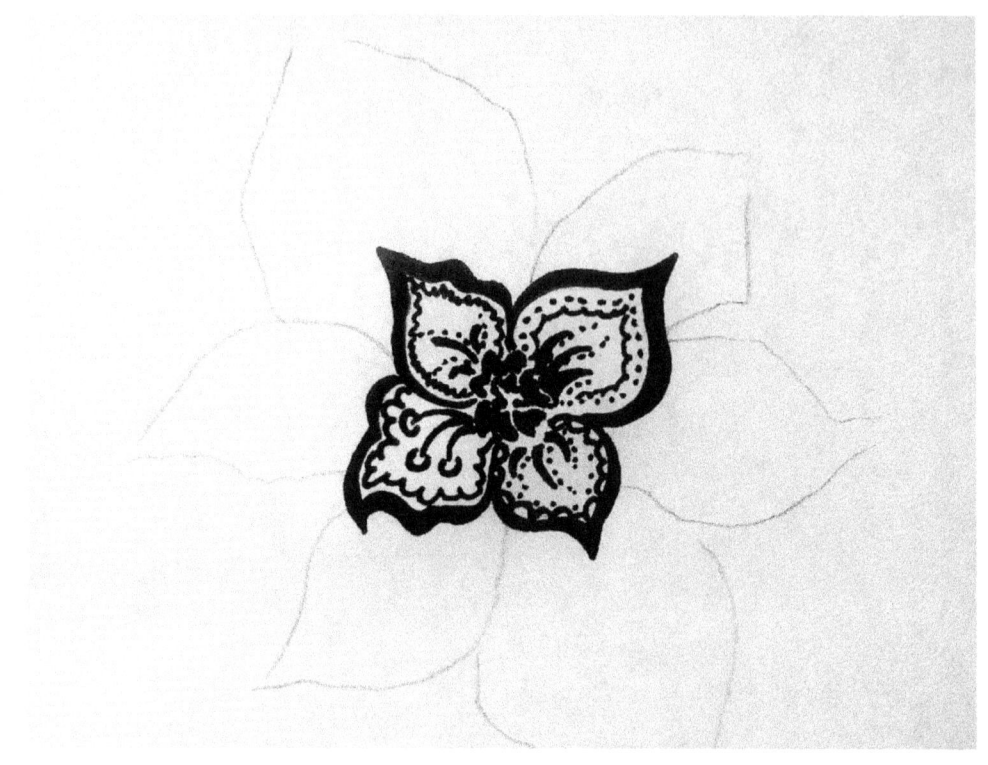

Step 4: Once more, draw more rose petals. Continue sketching them out and you will begin to see a flower sprout.

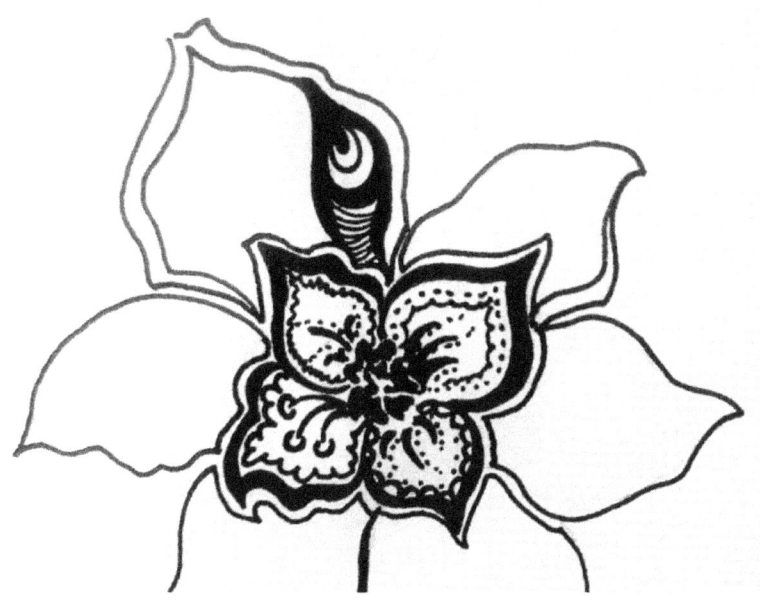

Step 5: Presently you will complete up the sketching so as to draw out whatever remains of the petals. This is the place you ought to delete the oversights you may have made to tidy up your rose.

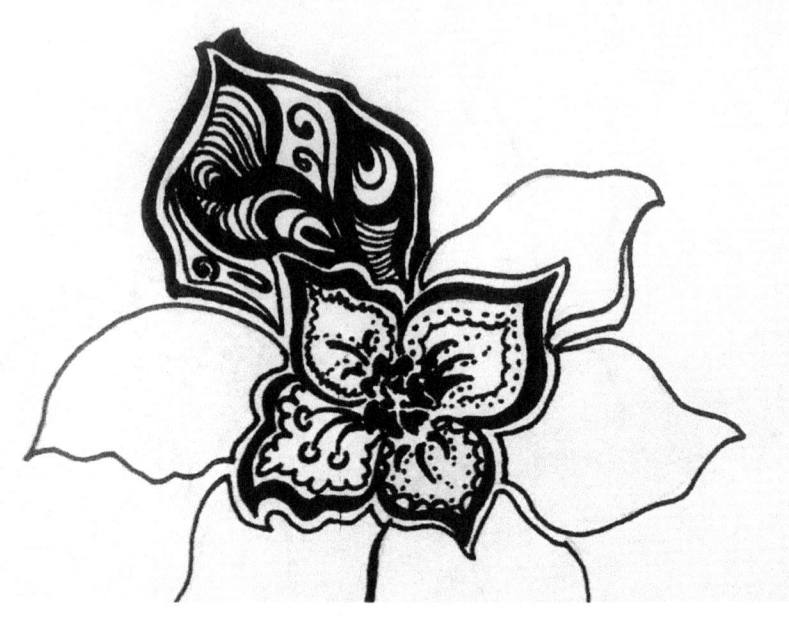

Step 6: Up next, draw three leaves ensuring that the edges are serrated.

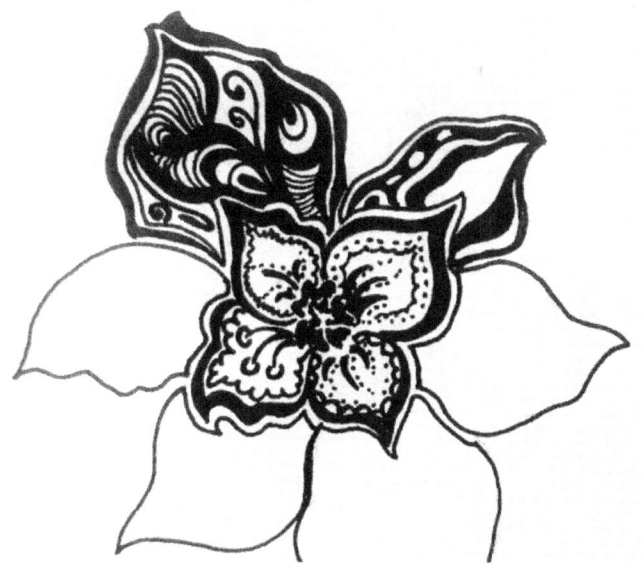

Step 7: Add specifying to the leaves and after that move along to step eight.

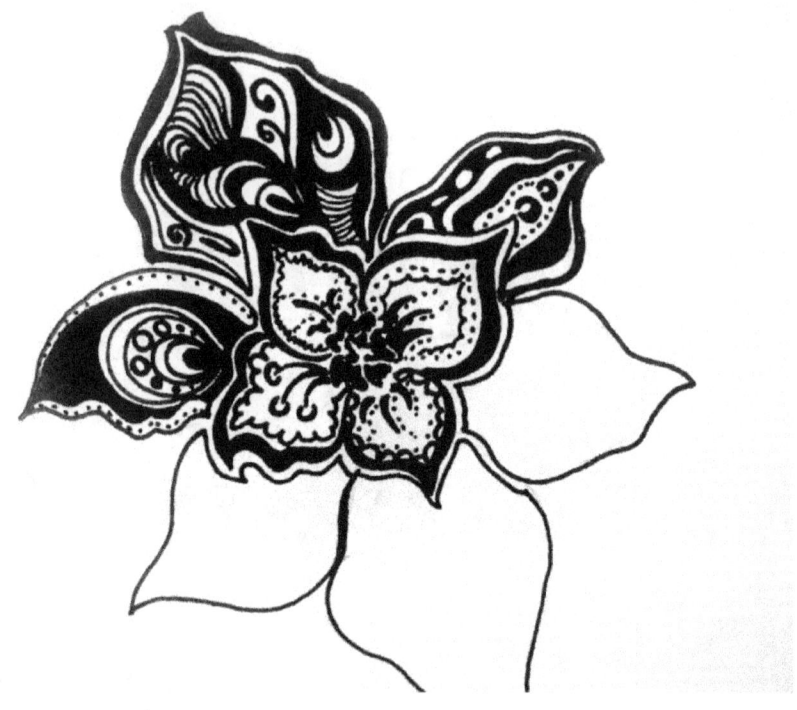

Step 8: We will now draw a few thistles like along these lines, and you can pick any thistle outline you like.

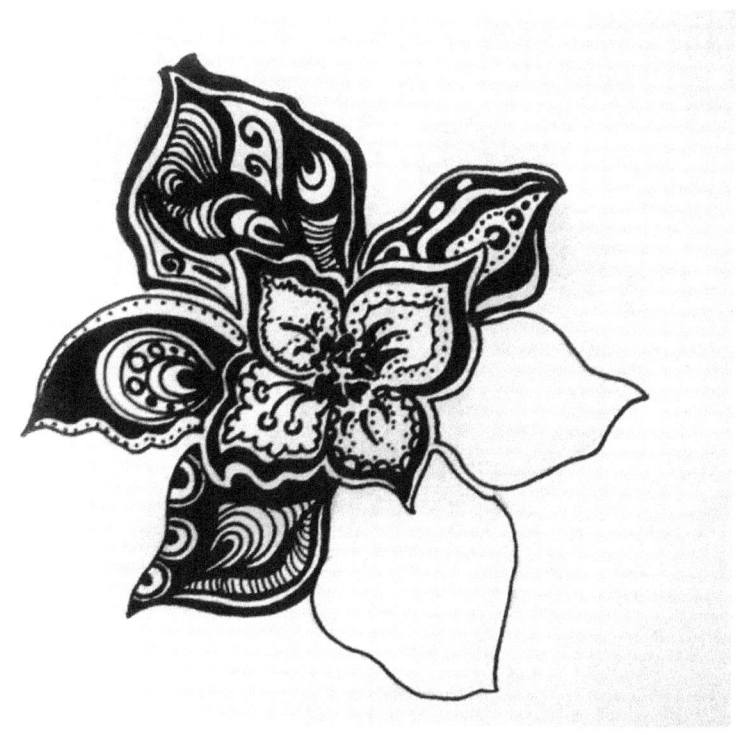

Step 9: Finally, include a few dots everywhere throughout the thistles.

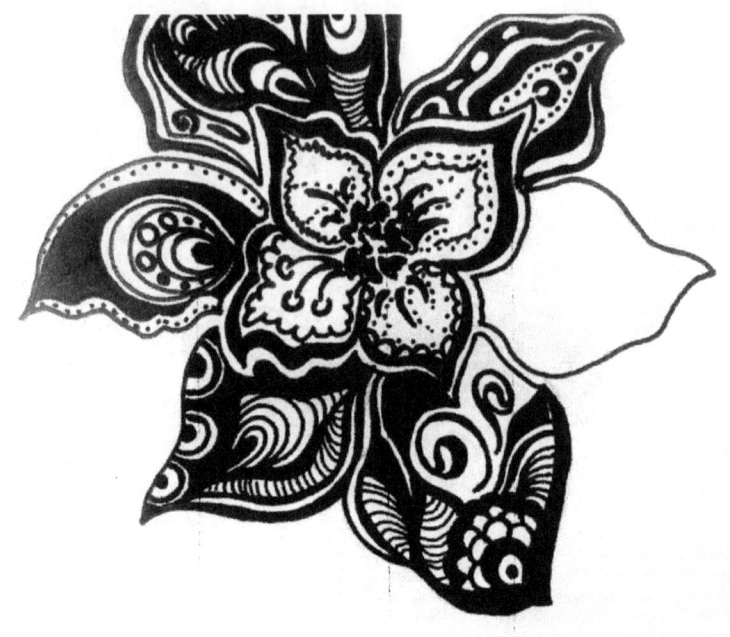

Step 10: This is the last step so you can delete botches when you are content with the drawing.

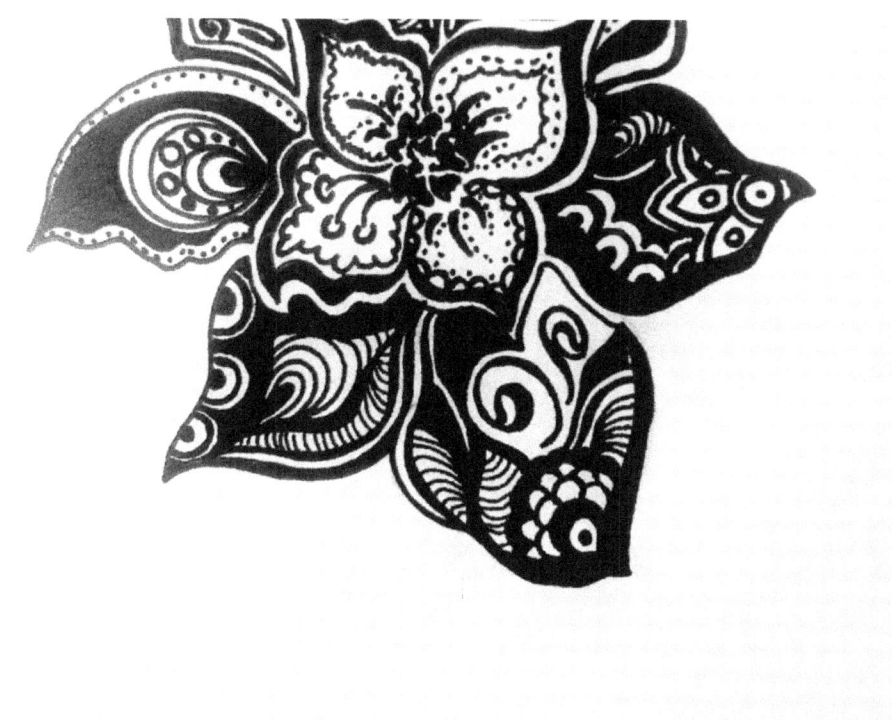

Step 11: Color in your Gothic rose and hotshot your work.

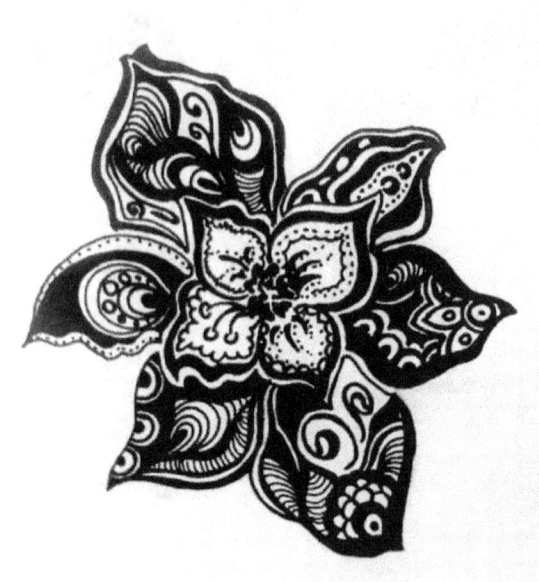

Step 12: Additionally make sure to present your got done with drawing when done too so others can look at the abilities.

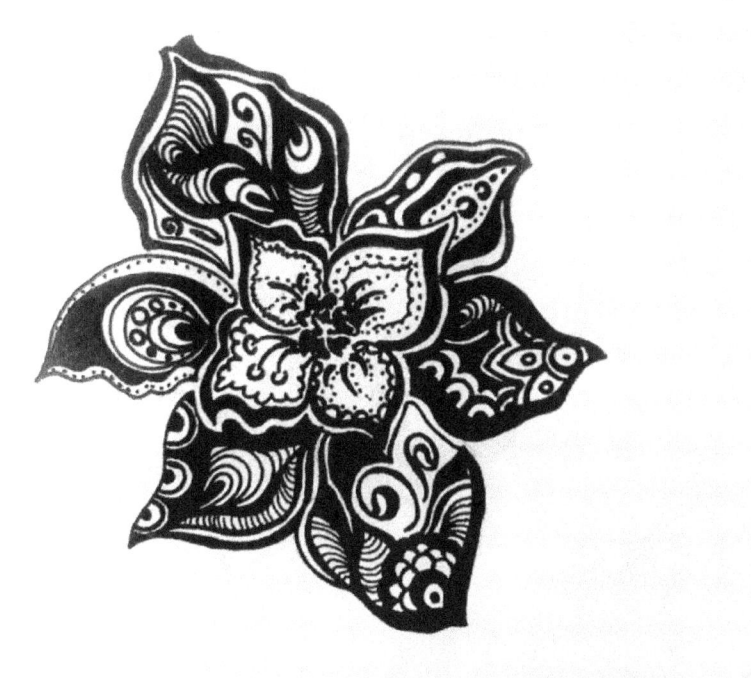

Step 13: Work on the shading part inside the flower.

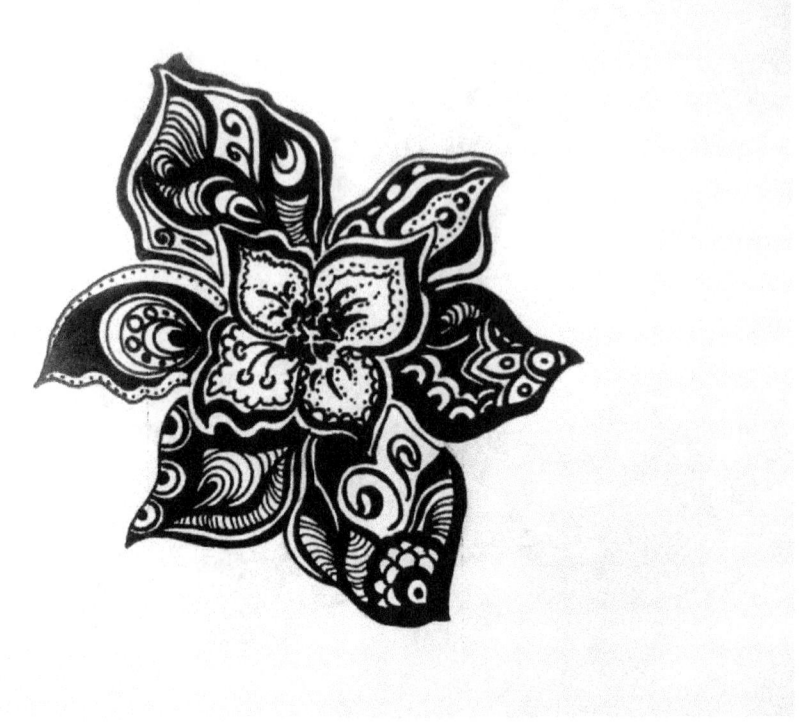

Step 14: If you think you are completed and you have done the necessary thing, work on the last step.

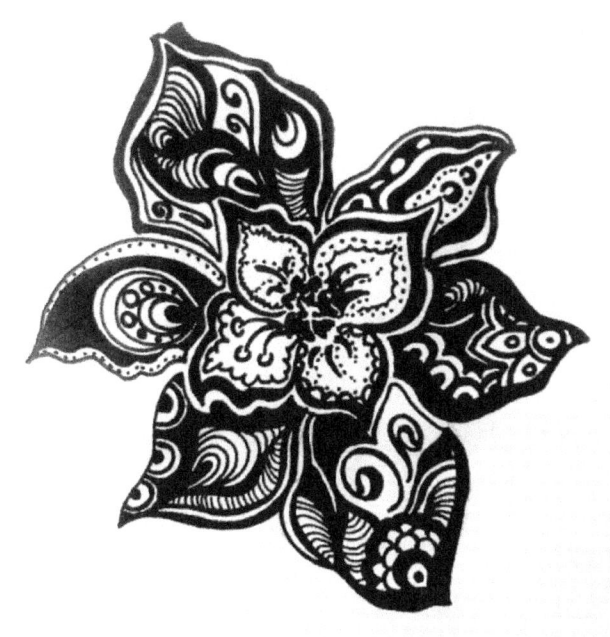

Step 15: Now you can sketch dark the parts which you want to highlight in the flower.

Chapter 5 – How to draw flower

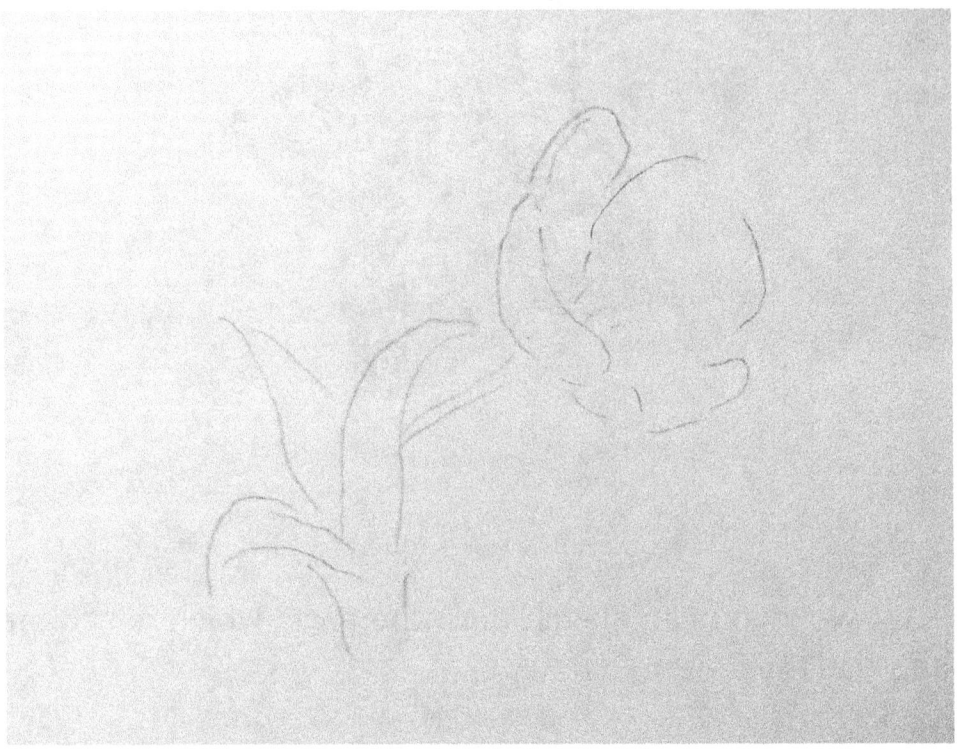

Step 1: Making an Easter lily will be truly fun. You should simply begin off making a circle for the middle aide of the flower.

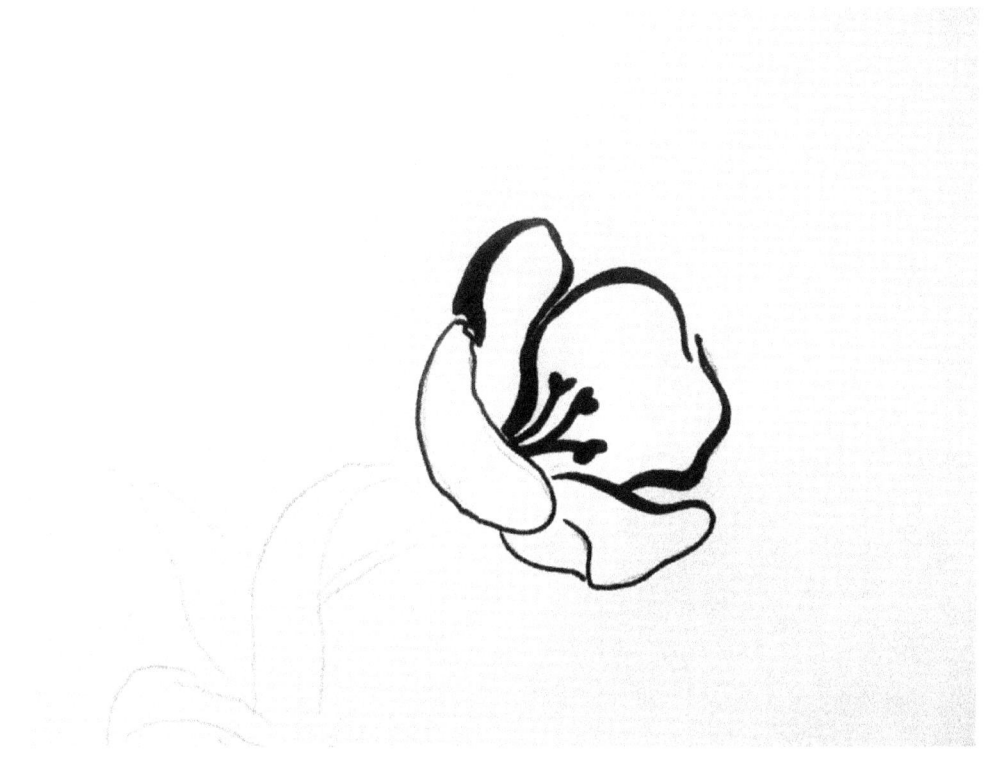

Step 2: Next, draw two petals of the trumpet molded flower like so. At this stage it looks more like sharp edges from a house fan.

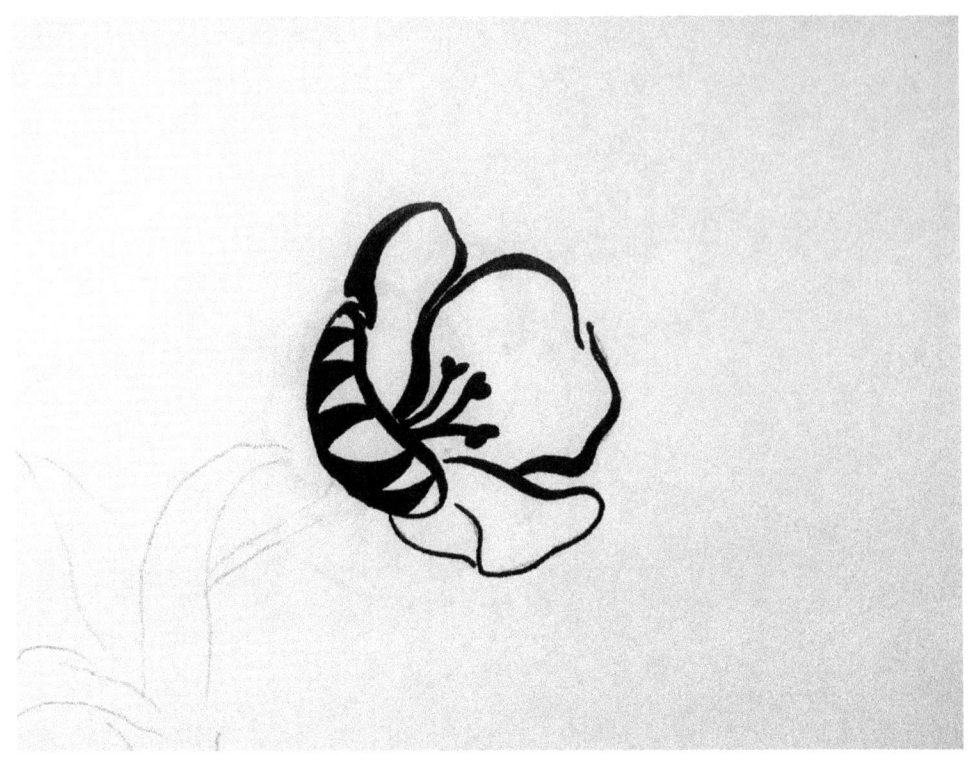

Step 3: Include two more petals like thus, and notice how the coating is smooth, and delicate streaming.

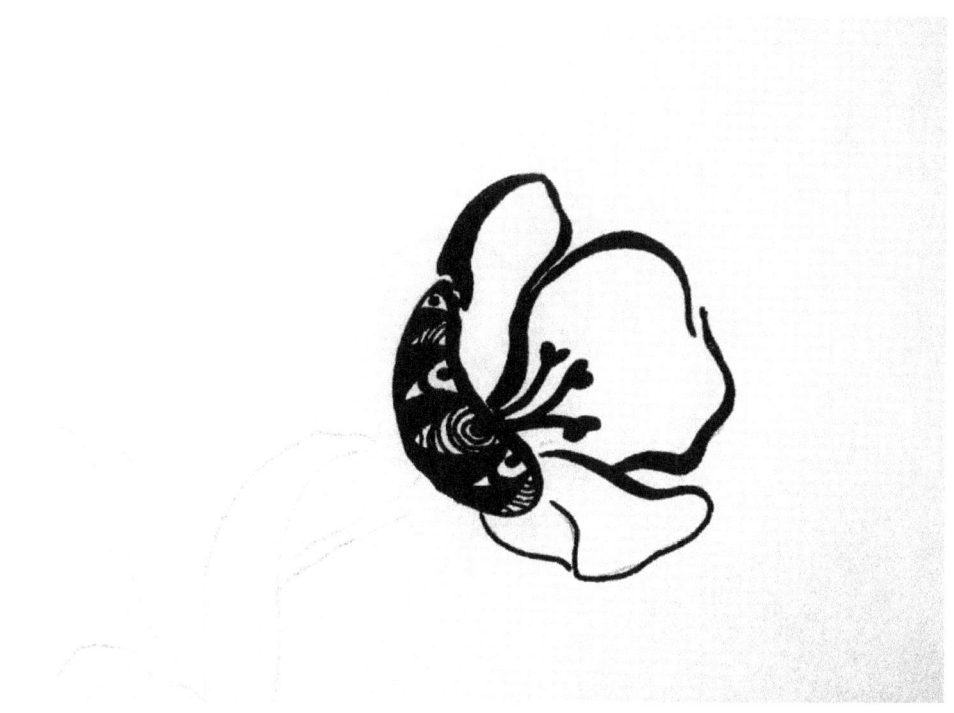

Step 4: Two more Easter lily petals are included between the others like so. This shouldn't be an issue to duplicate, yet in the event that you feel that you can't draw the petals effectively, simply take as much time as is needed and sketch them out rather than hard squeeze drawing them.

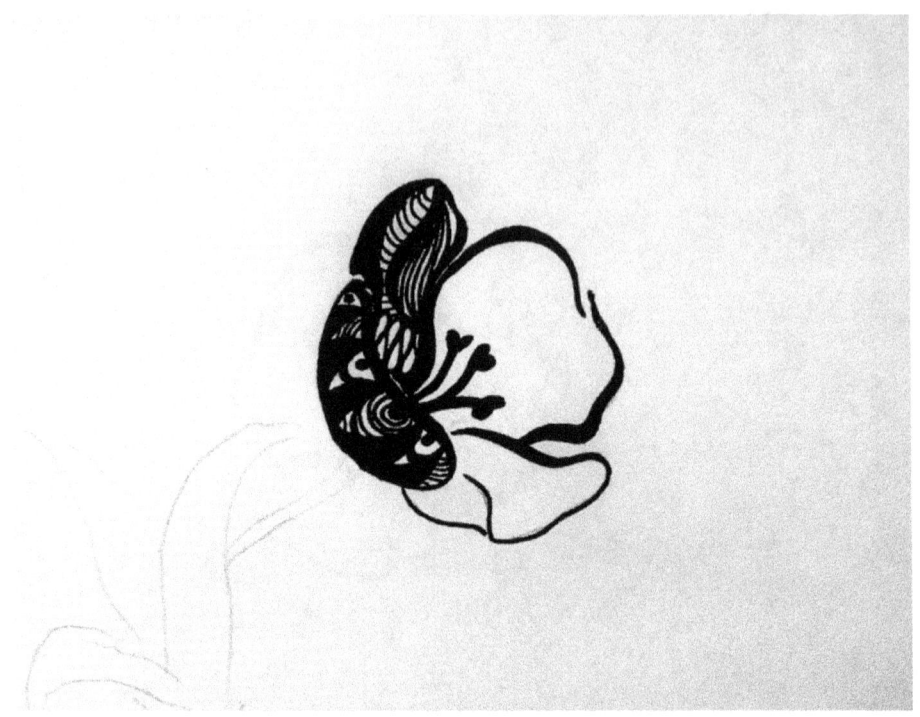

Step 5: The fun begins now on the grounds that we will be transforming a conventional looking flower idea into something delightful and conspicuous. Sketch in focus lines down the center of every petal like so. At the point when that is done you can include the stamens in the focal point of the lily like so.

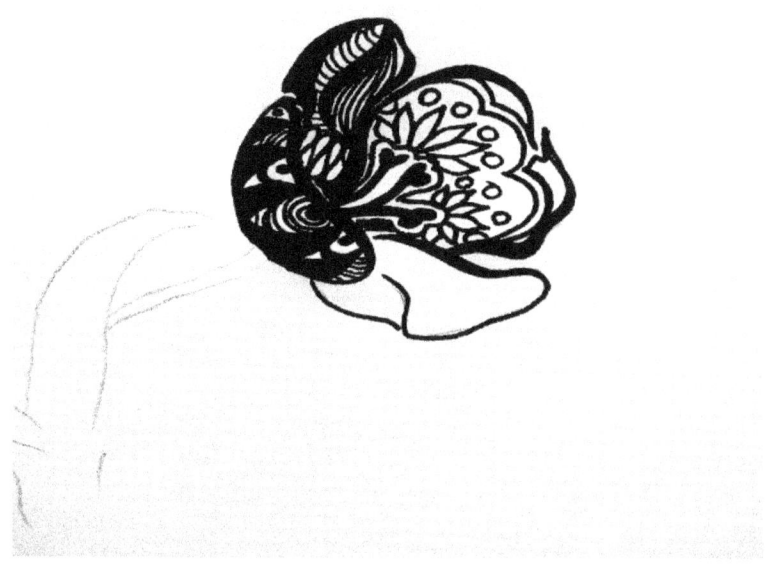

Step 6: You will now begin sketching out the horn shape that is consistently joined to the sprout like so. The base some portion of the flower streams specifically into the stem of the Easter lily like you see here. Draw in the long, grass like leaves like along these lines, then tidy up the drawing to flawlessness.

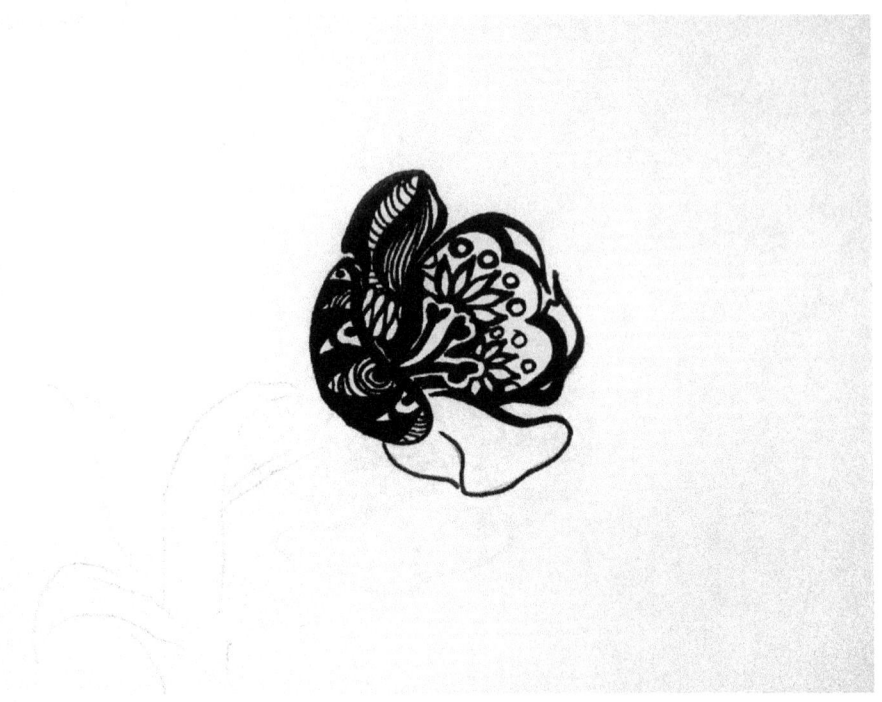

Step 7: Here is the thing that your flower ought to turn out looking like when you are all done.

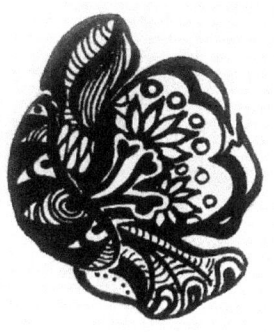

Step 8: Color in the sprout utilizing white and green shades. Presently you have yourself an Easter lily that was drawn by you!

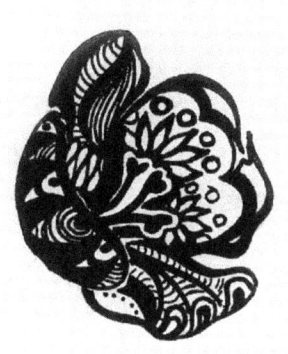

Step 9: Next, start drawing in all the stamen of the lily which discards from the focal point of the flower. The tips, which are called anthers ought to be drawn in an oval formed way.

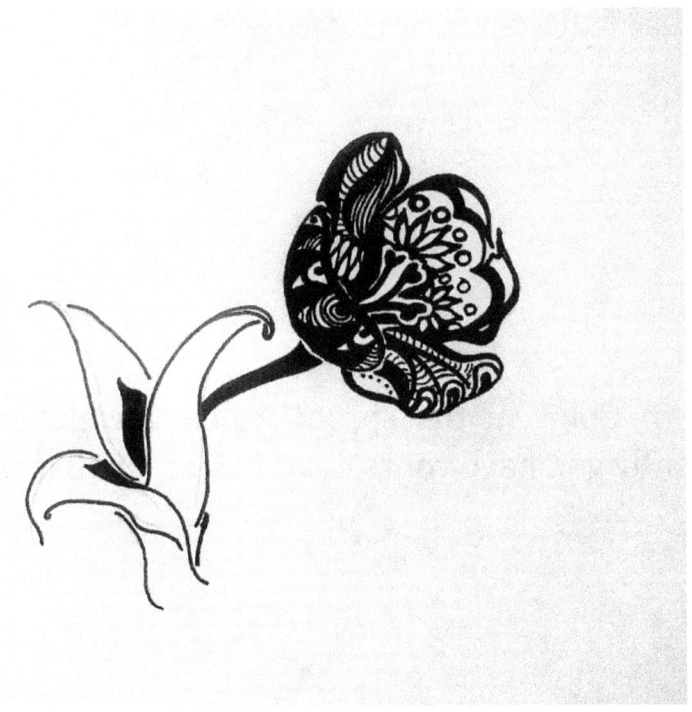

Step 10: Presently you can start drawing out the flower petals. They ought to be elliptical formed and tapper at the closures. The edging ought to be somewhat wavy too.

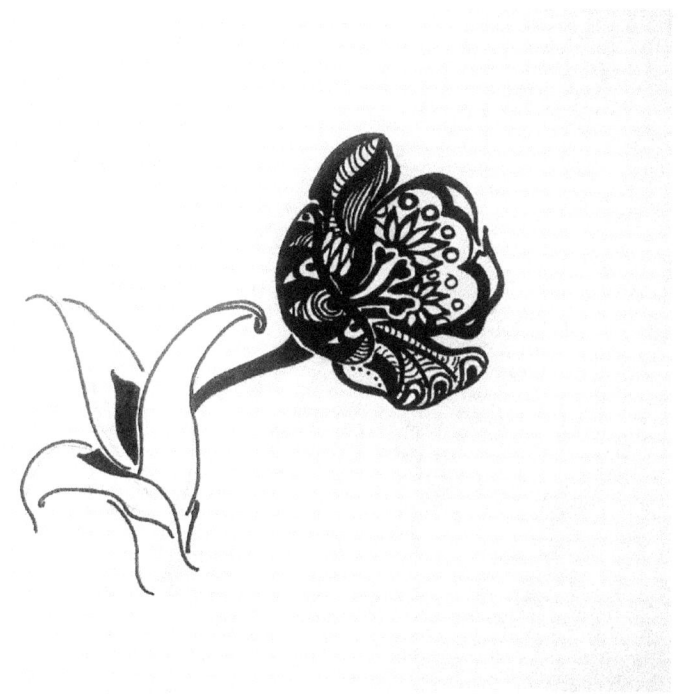

Step 11: Draw three petals for the time being, then when you are done move to step four.

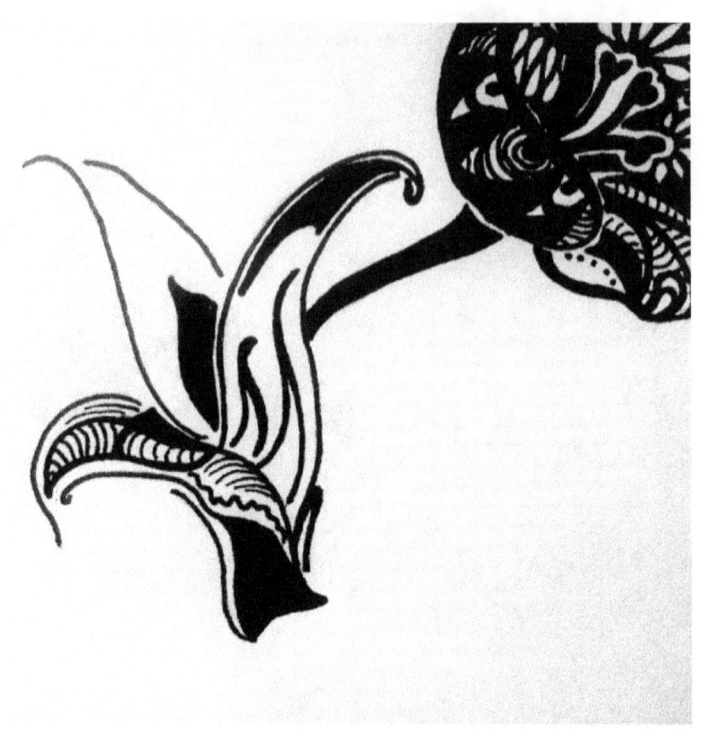

Step 12: You will now draw the last three petals for your Stargazer lily. Notice how the coating is fixed.

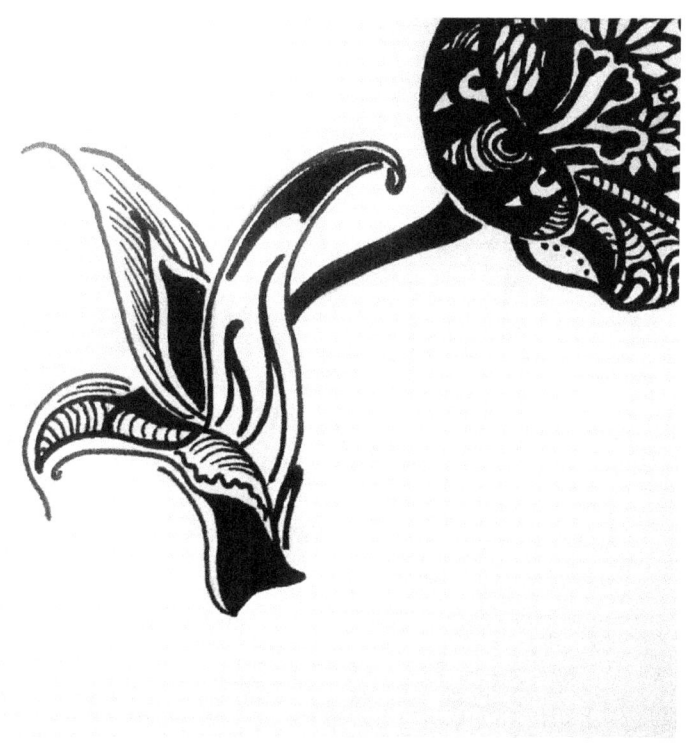

Step 13: Twist in the tips for every petal then move along to step five where you will complete this flower off.

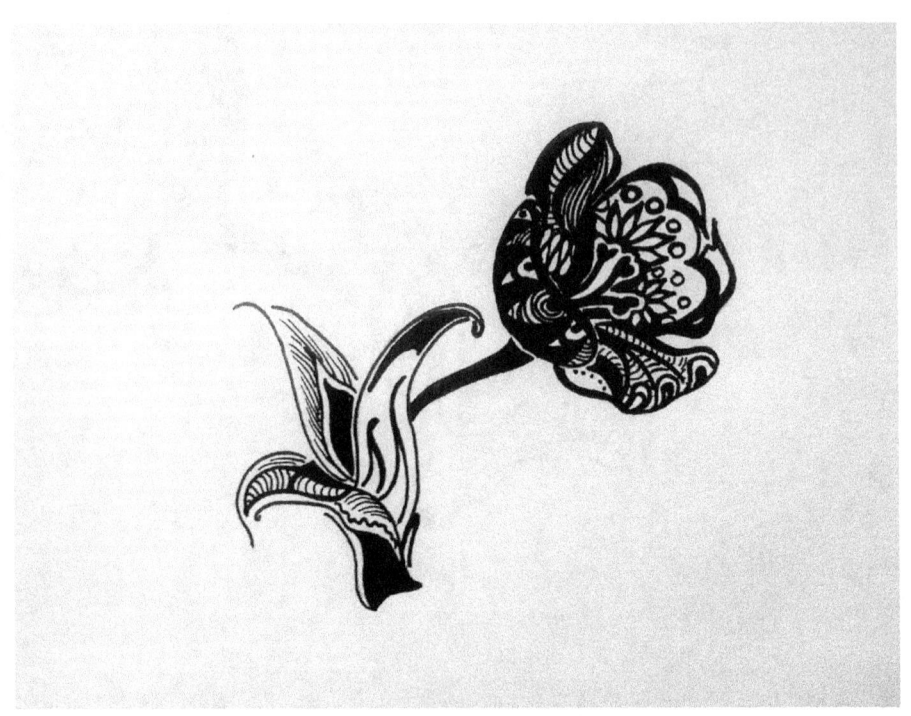

Step 14: Sketch in the middle lines that detail the flower. When this has been done, you can begin deleting your missteps.

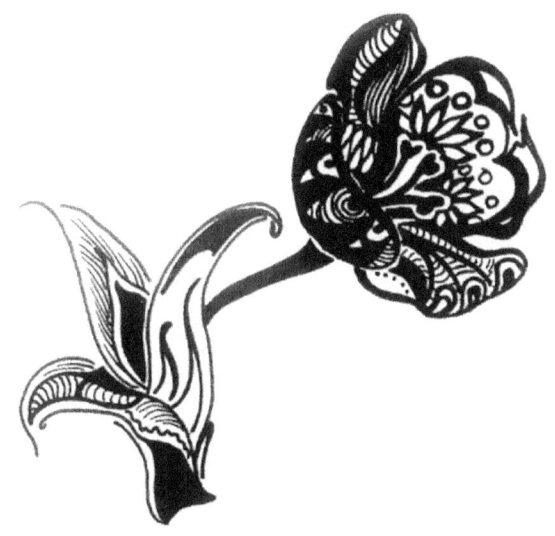

Step 15: Color in your Stargazer lily utilizing the fundamental colored picture as a source of perspective, or discover your own one of a kind photo of a Stargazer for a coloring aide.

Chapter 6 – How to draw butterfly

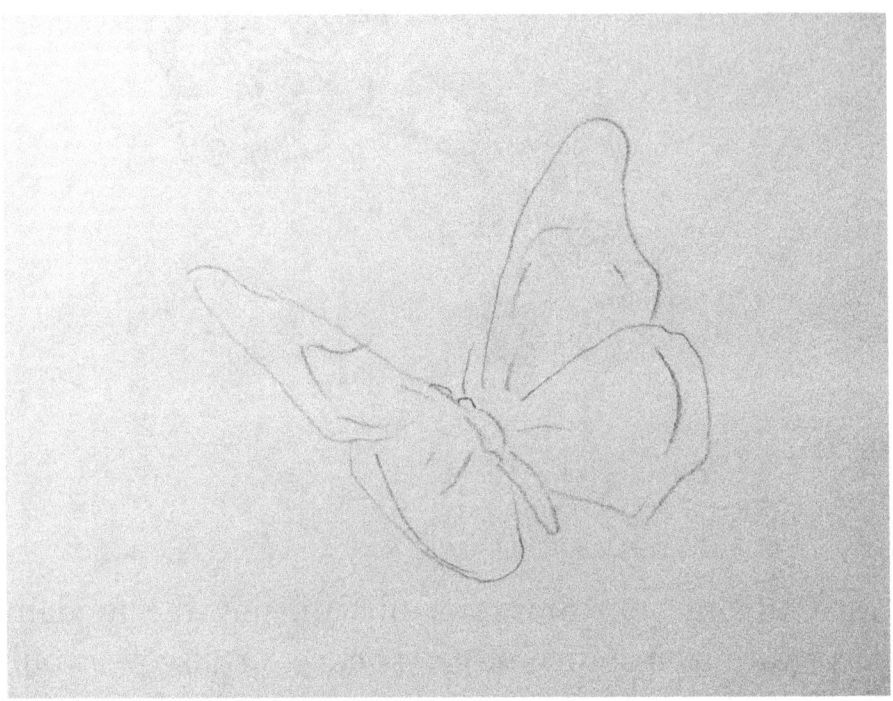

Step 1: Like the sheriff skull you will begin this progression with a couple of straight rules. Draw one vertical line down the center of your paper. Next draw four flat lines that vary long.

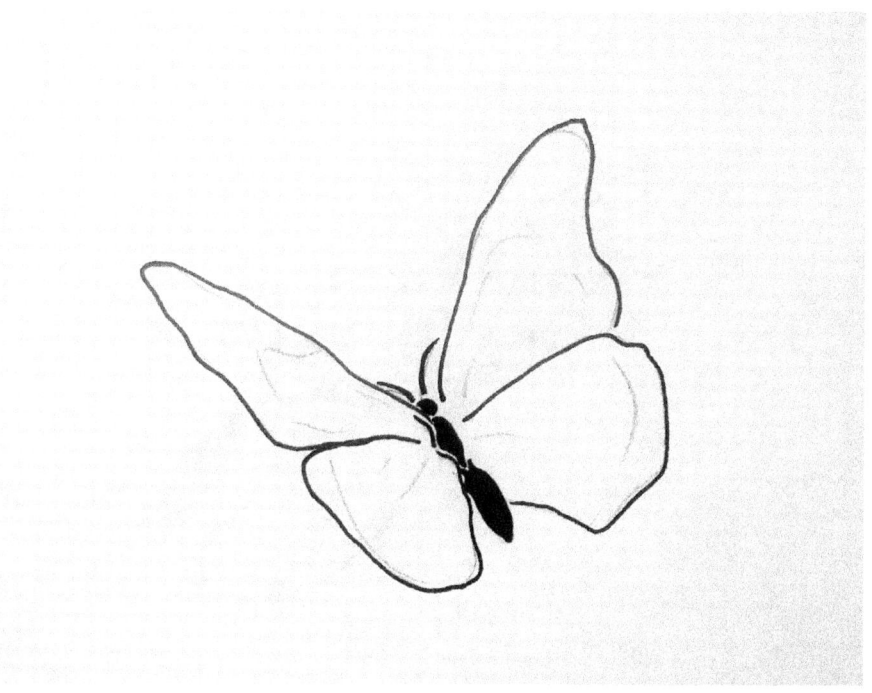

Step 2: Step two is really straightforward too. All you will be doing is drawing out the delineated state of the butterfly.

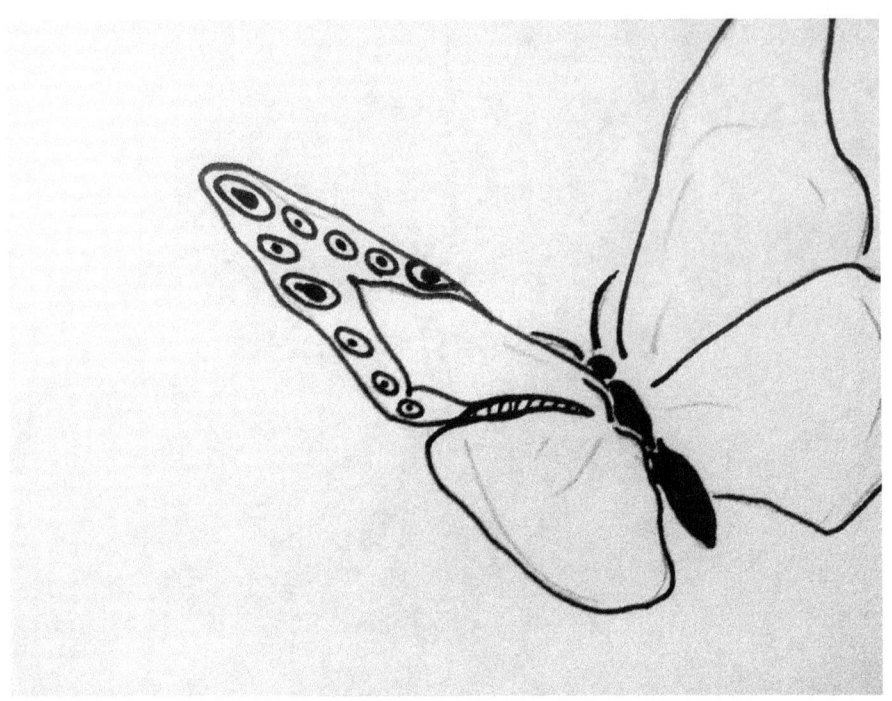

Step 3: This is the place you can adjust the style of butterfly you need. When your butterfly is drawn out utilizing the rules you drew as a part of step one, you can move to the following step.

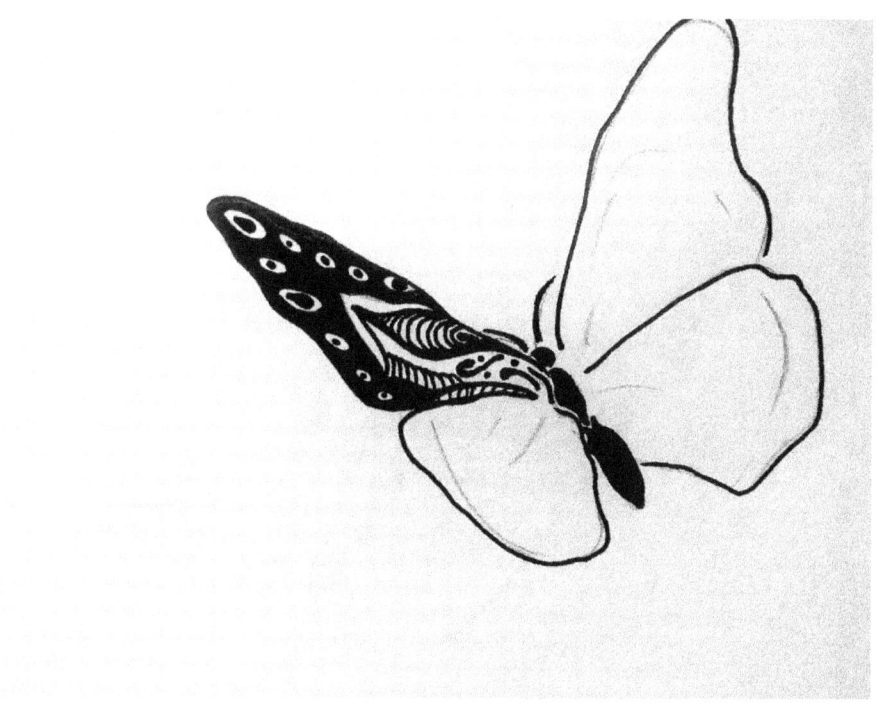

Step 4: Presently this is the place the stride gets fun. To begin with draw another illustrated plan around the butterfly wings.

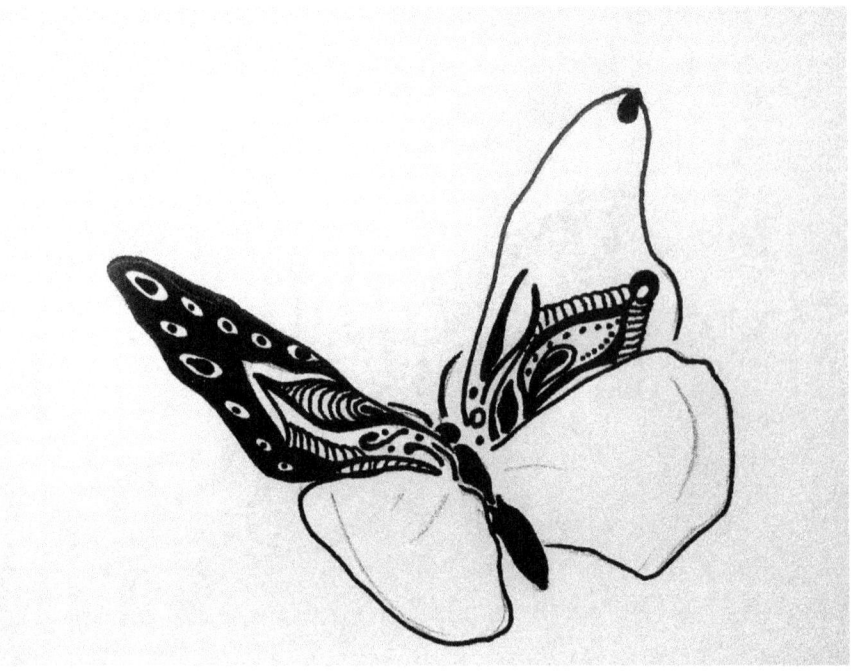

Step 5: Next draw the shape and style of the eyes that will make your butterfly eyes look excellent and interesting.

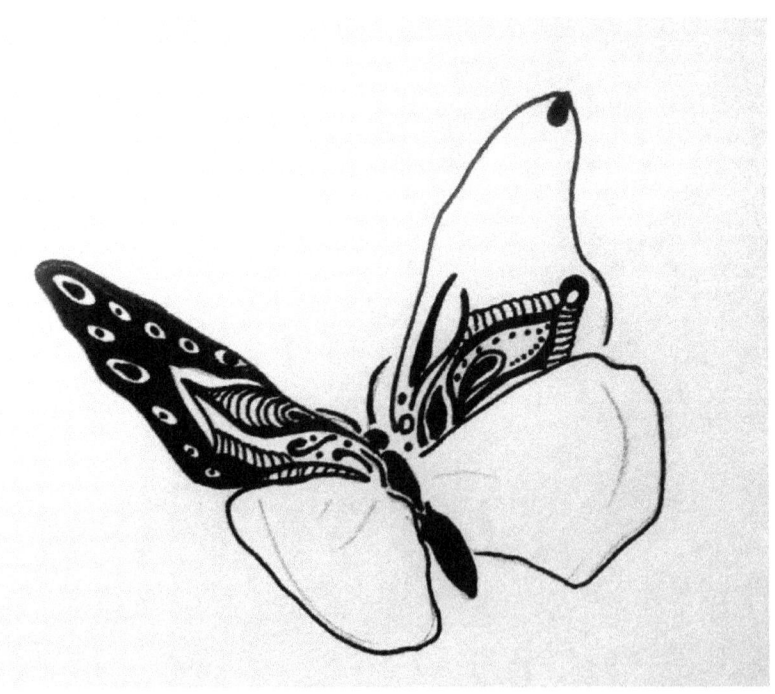

Step 6: This is the last drawing step and you should simply draw out the radio wires, and leg like shapes under the center of the body. Give the butterfly his own eyes and after that include some itemizing and outline.

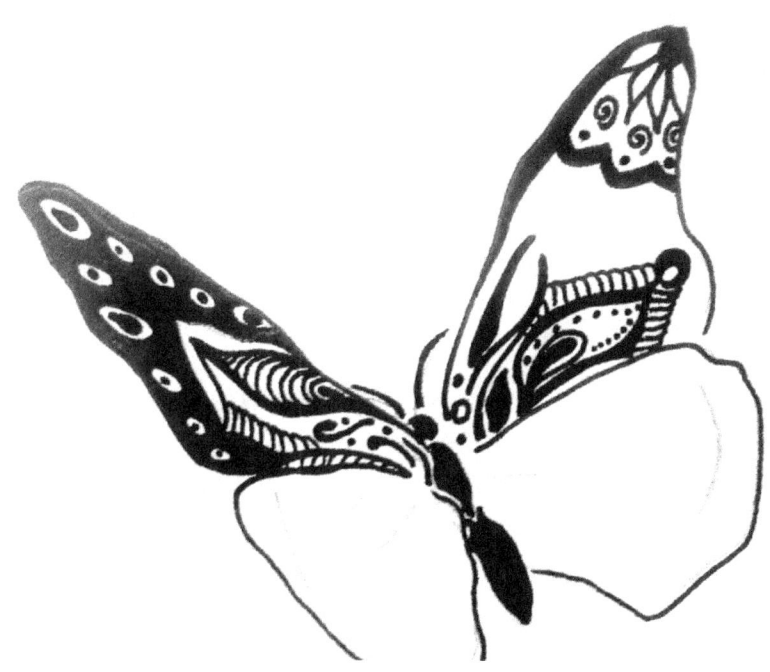

Step 7: This is the thing that your configuration and drawing ought to look like when you are finished.

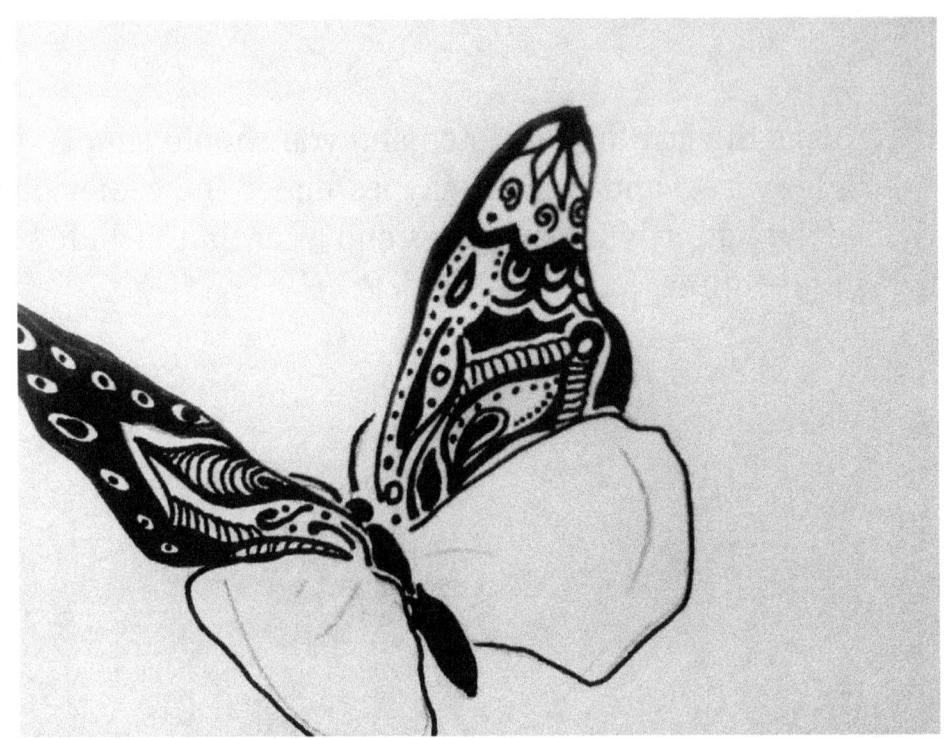

Step 8: All you need to do now is color the eyes and butterfly in utilizing the shades you like best. Learning how to draw butterfly eyes orderly was fun and energizing. I trust you all had a great time also.

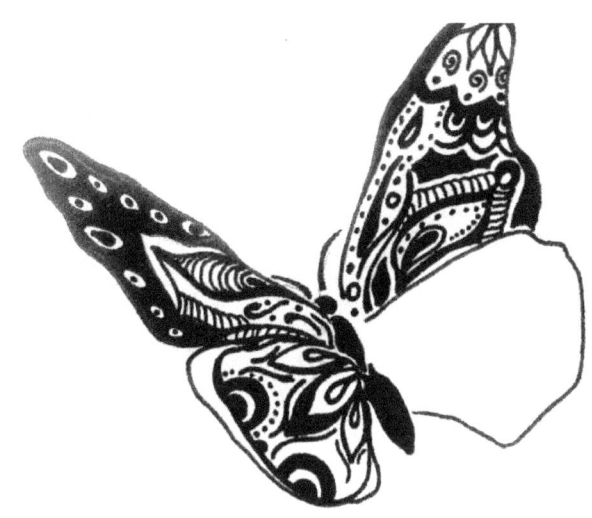

Step 9: Begin this initial step by drawing the state of the butterfly wings and afterward a circle shape off to the lower left hand side for the heart. Ensure you take as much time as necessary so that all the coating turns out pleasant and flawless.

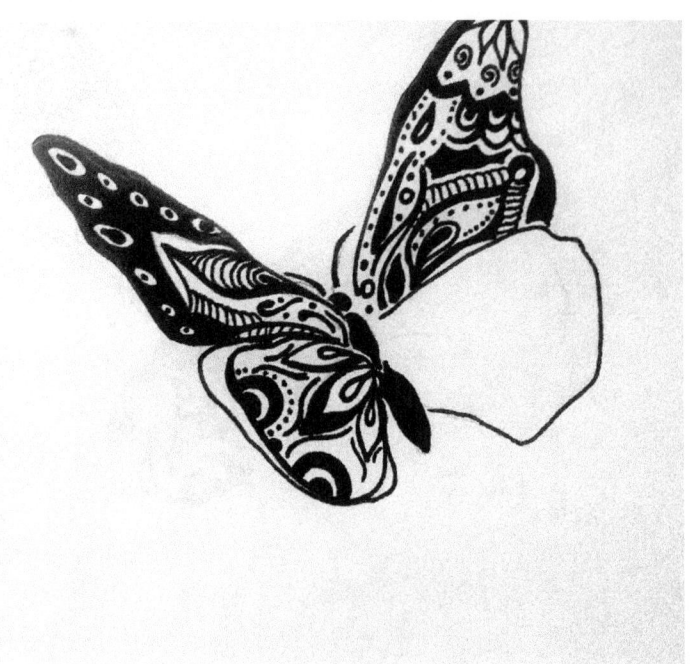

Step 10: See this lesson isn't too terrible right? You will now begin sketching out the genuine state of the butterfly wings as you see here. They have curves and indicates make them pretty and dainty looking.

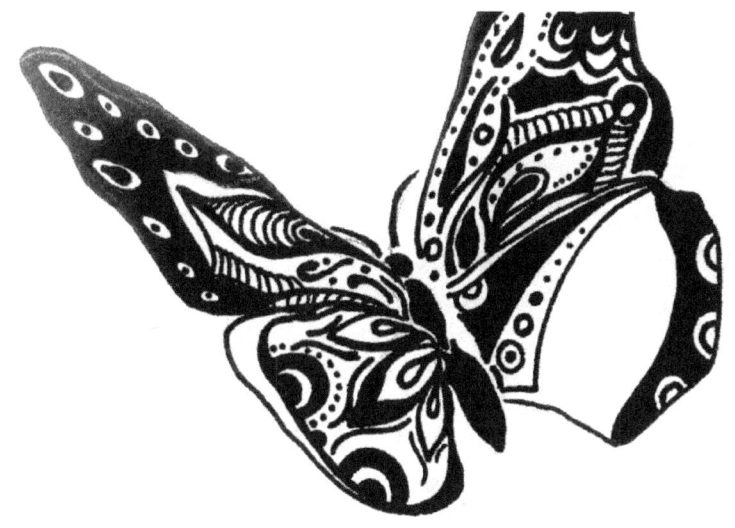

Step 11: You will then draw out the state of the bug body and afterward include one line at the finishes of every wing. You will then draw out the beginning state of the heart too.

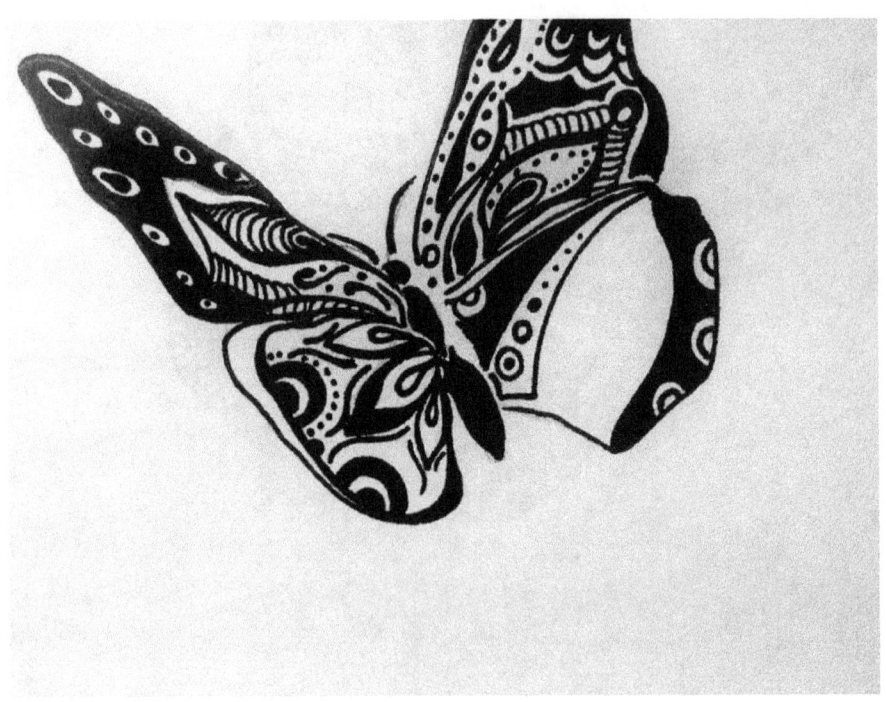

Step 12: Presently as should be obvious you have made it to your third step which implies you are practically done. Presently as should be obvious you will take as much time as is needed adding the lovely plan to the butterfly wings and after that thicken the lower tips also. You will then include some receiving wire lines and after that eyeballs.

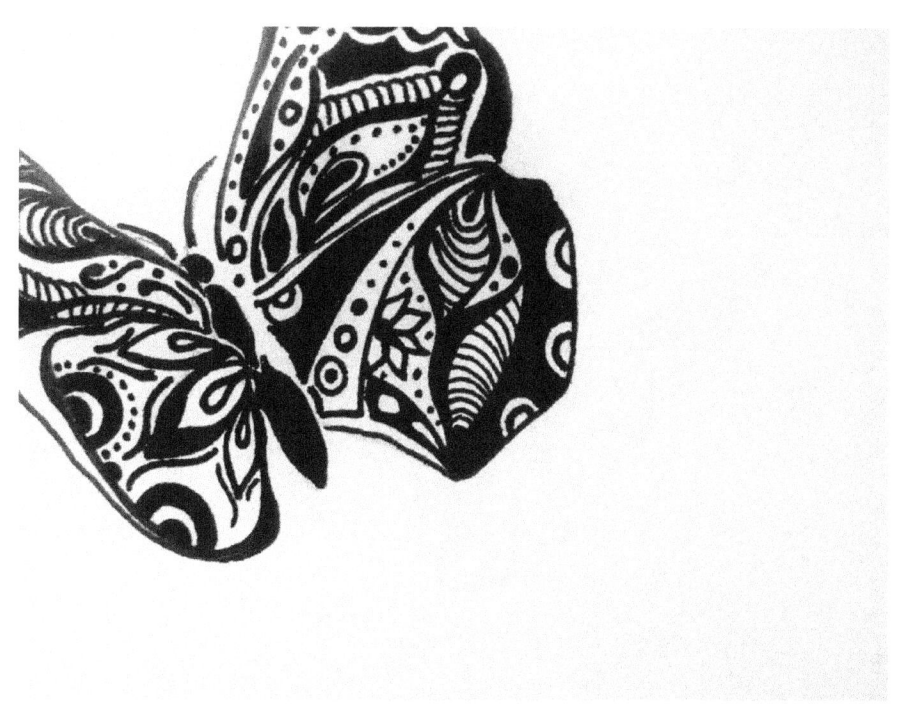

Step 13: Well you have made it to your last step and here you will complete the wing configuration on your delightful butterfly. You can then delete every one of your rules and shapes that you attracted step one.

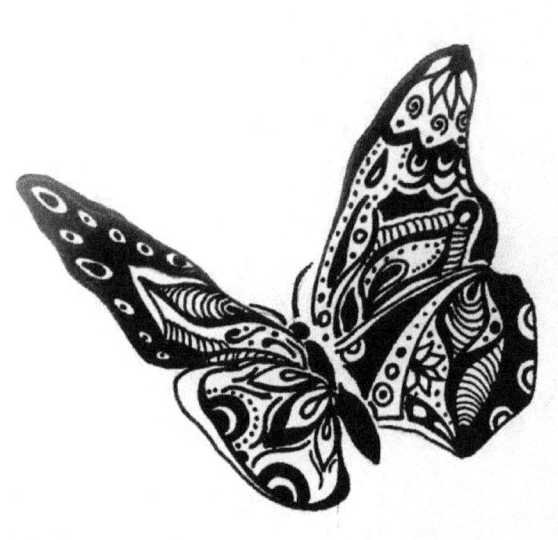

Step 14: Ta da! This is precisely what your completed tattoo outline looks like when you are completely done. I trust you preferred this instructional exercise on the most proficient method to draw butterfly plans regulated.

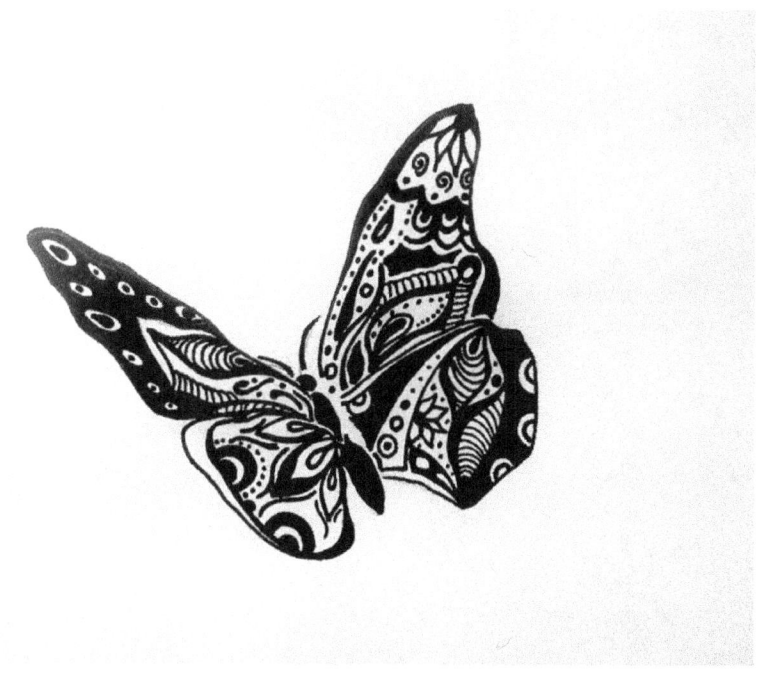

Step 15: Now you can sketch the parts which are necessary.

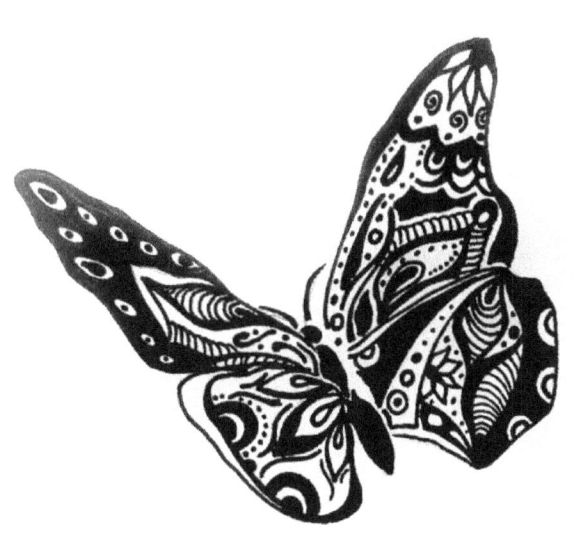

Step 16: Now just make sure that you have shaded the parts darkly.

Chapter 7 – How to draw flower

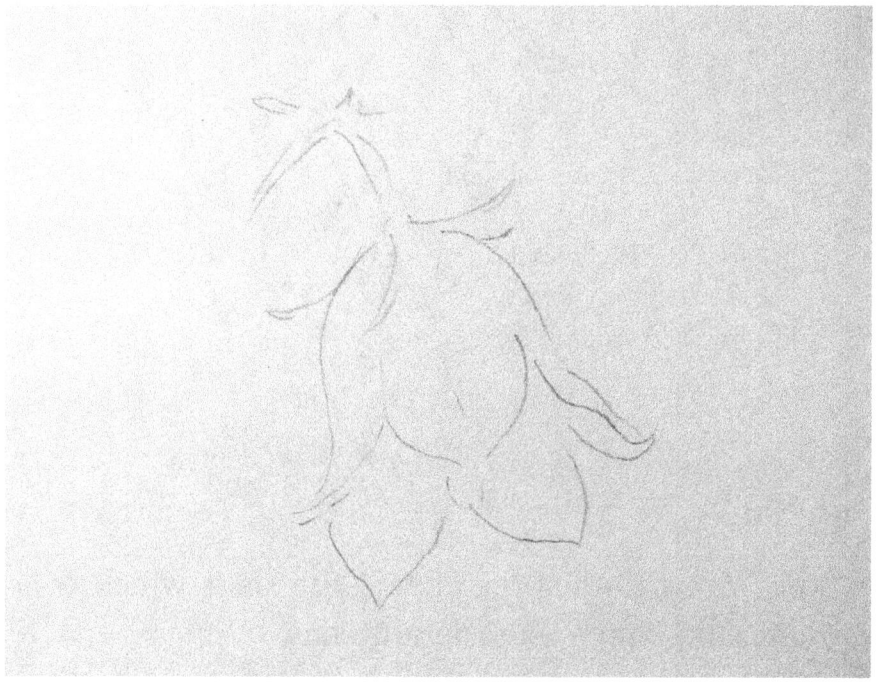

Step 1: Make an oval shape for the base of the tulip.

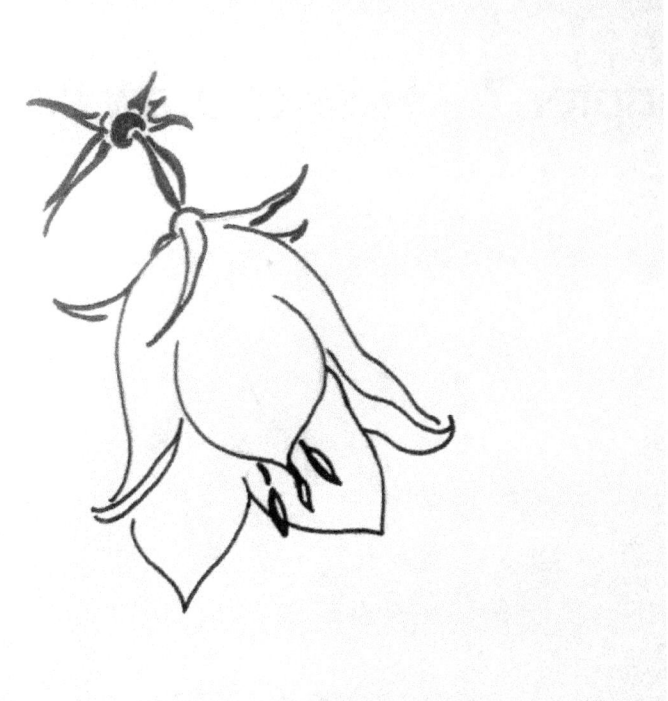

Step 2: Next, draw the two pedals on the sides which will frame that container like shape that the tulip has.

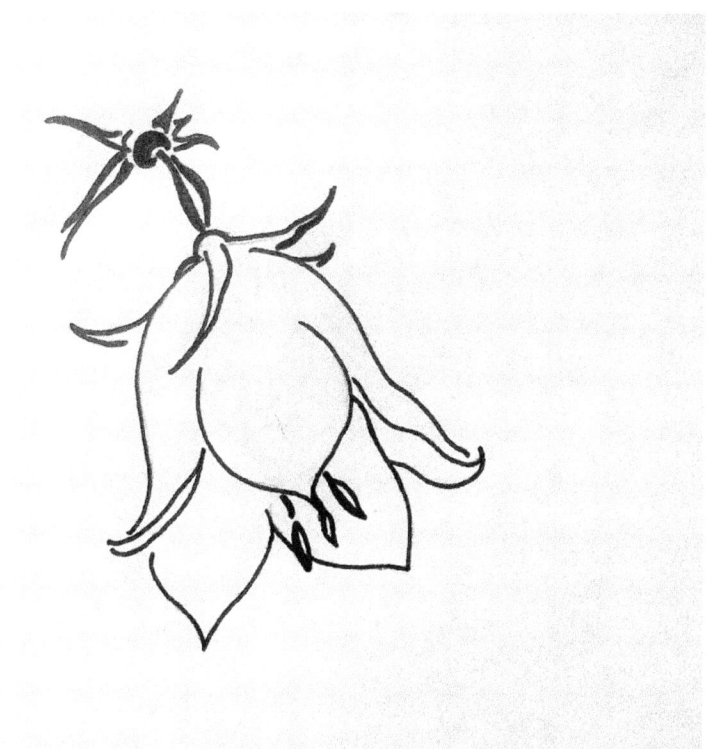

Step 3: Next, just draw in the tips of the other flower pedals to make the tulip look full or in sprout.

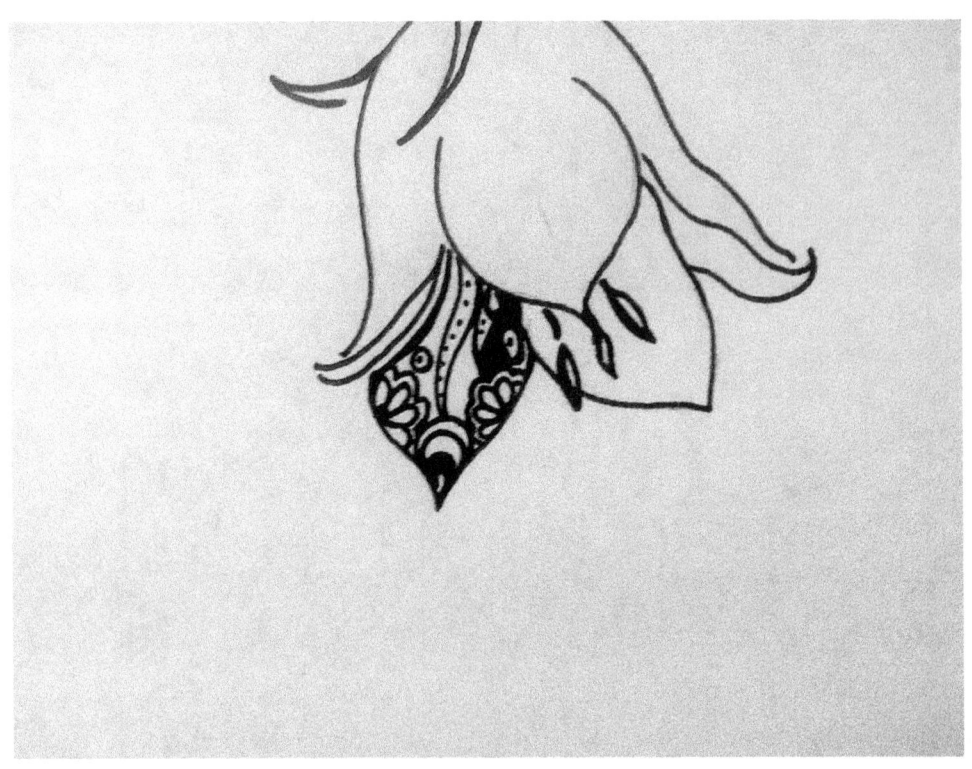

Step 4: In conclusion, simply draw a stem that tappers in transit down. Eradicate the mix-ups on the off chance that you made any.

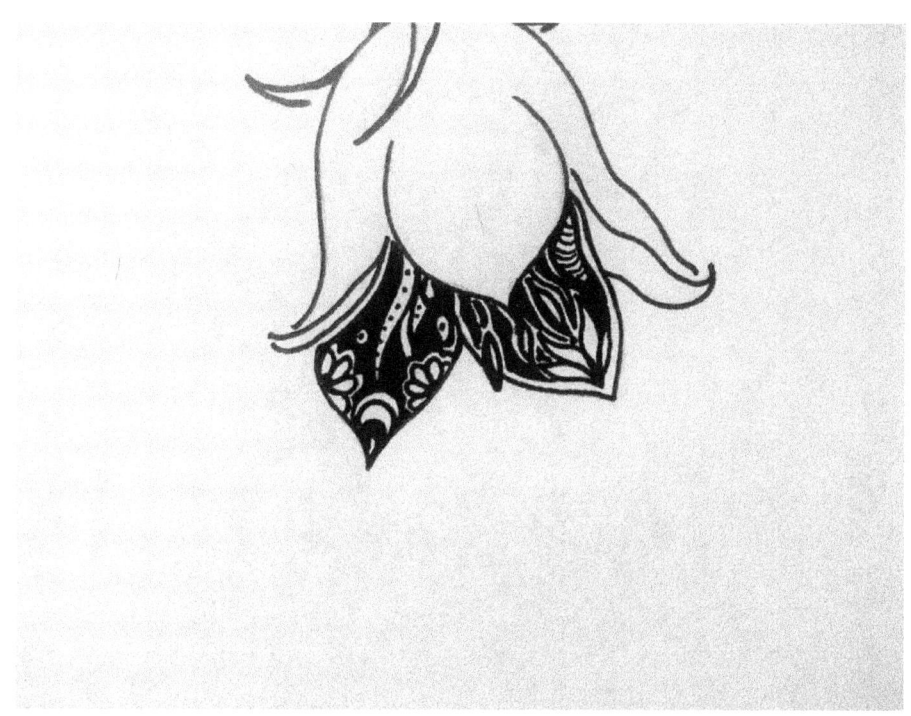

Step 5: Presently how about we begin shading. Begin at the base of the first pedal. The base ought to be the darkest piece of the pedal. As you work your way up the flower, the shading gets lighter.

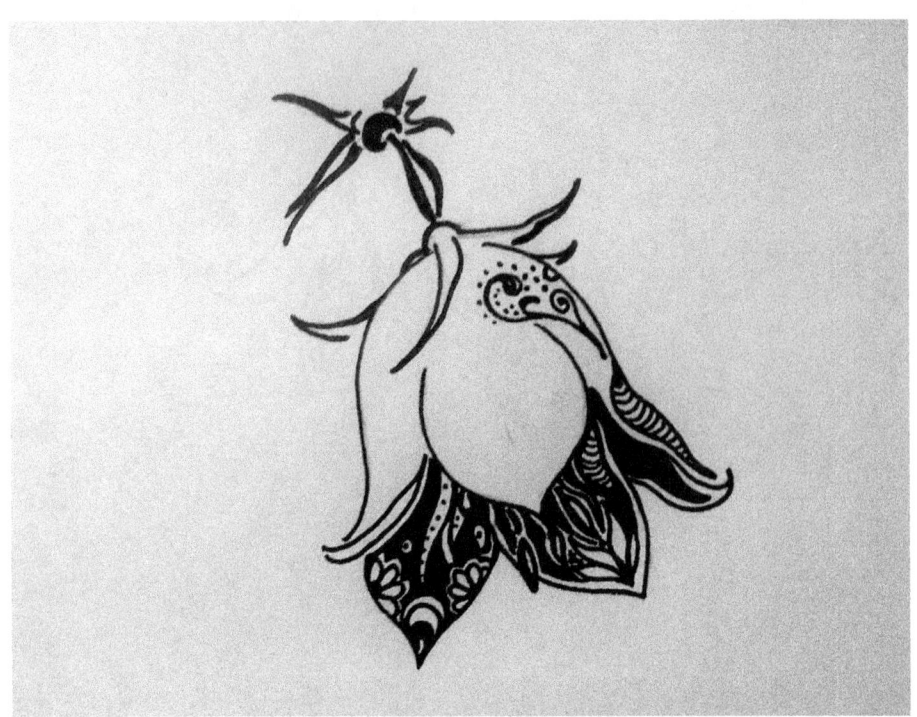

Step 6: Fill whatever is left of the pedals with the establishment like thus, making a point to do precisely.

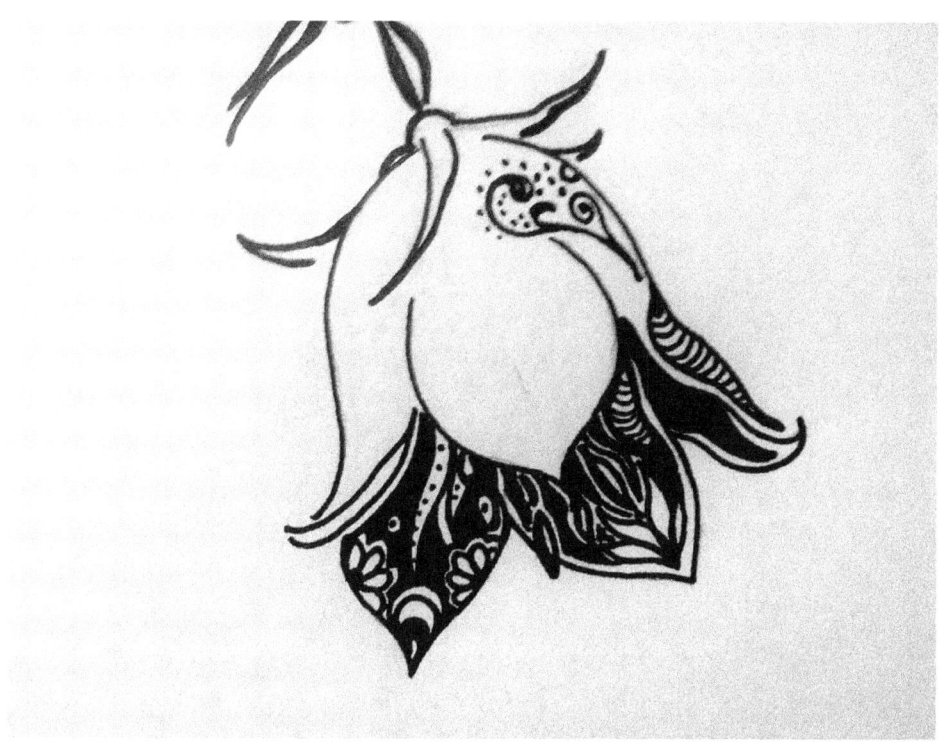

Step 7: Wrap up whatever is left of the tulip, then continue to step eight where you will include all the highlighting and composition itemizing.

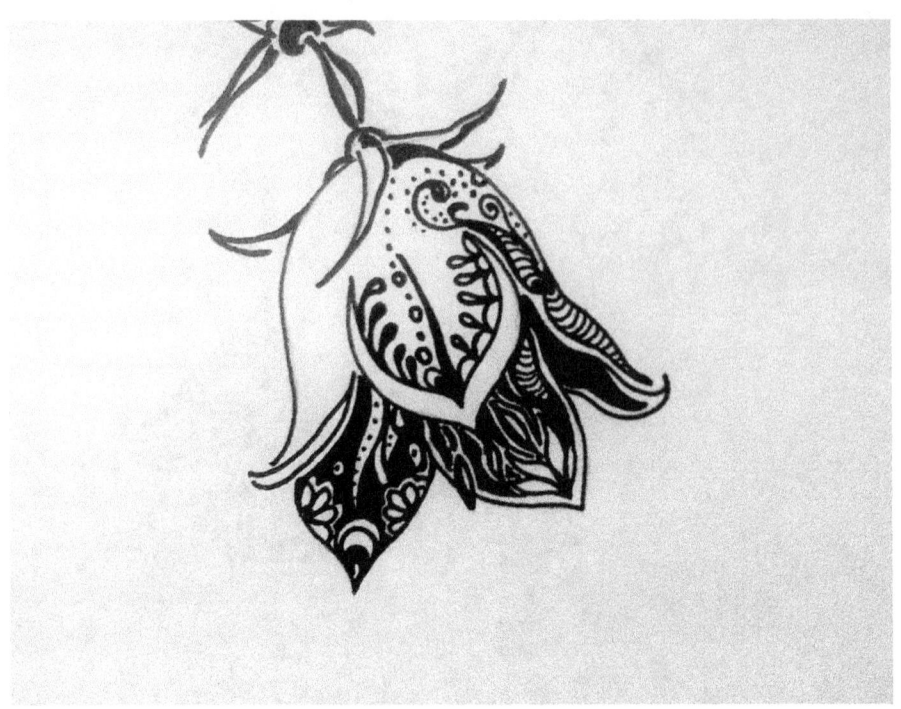

Step 8: Precisely eradicate the coating that makes the pedals look drawn. Try not to delete these lines totally, simply black out them out. At the point when that is done, mix in the surface and make the tips of the pedals the lightest of the entire flower.

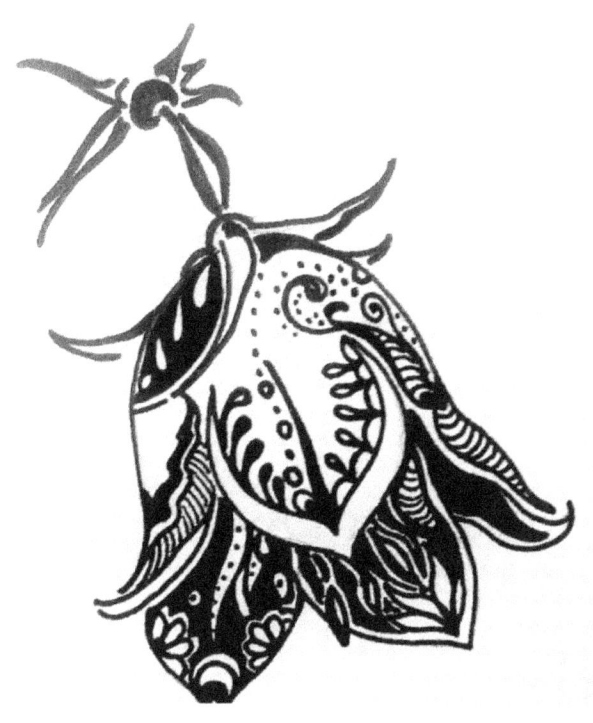

Step 9: Make two circles, one for every sprout. Make certain to draw them slantingly over one another.

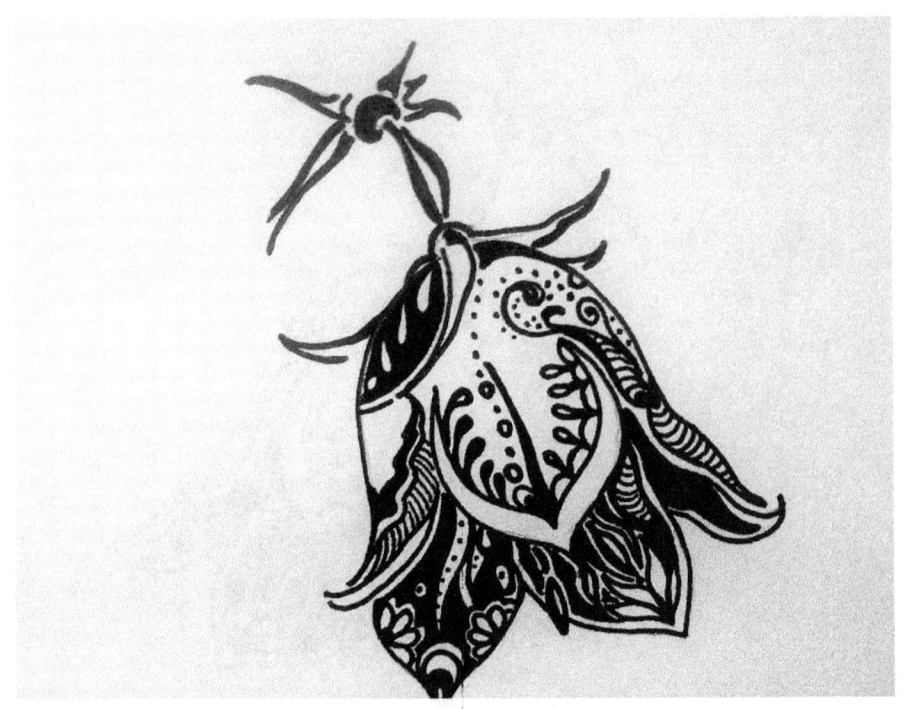

Step 10: Begin with the lily and draw out the four states of the flower petals. The tips of every petal is kind of level and thrilling.

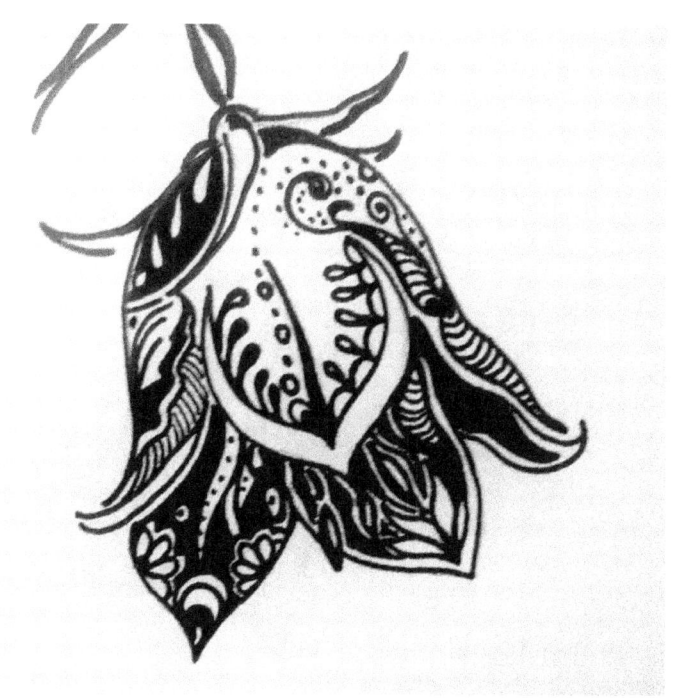

Step 11: This is likely going to be one of the least demanding roses you will draw. You need to draw a rose from the side perspective like so. Draw in a winding focus and have the external petal fold over.

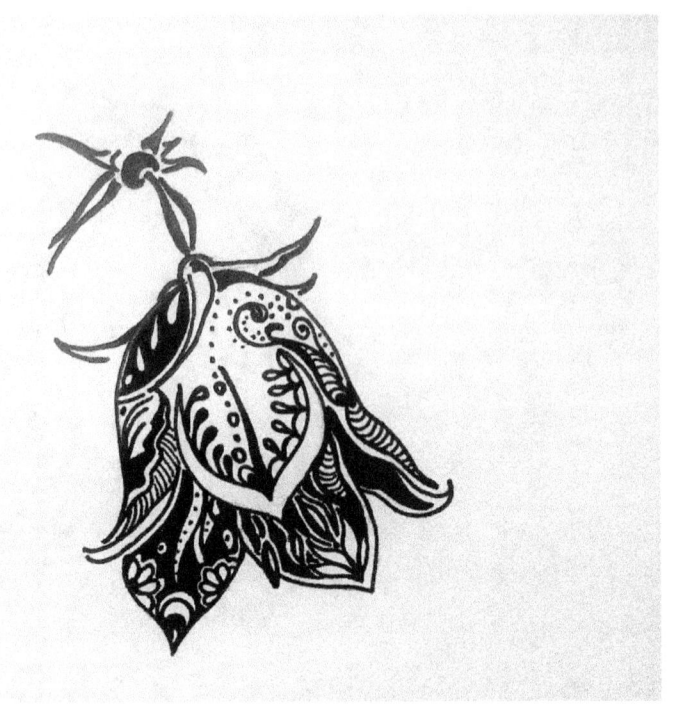

Step 12: Utilizing the other shape you attracted step one, you will draw in the five daffodil petals like in this way, and as should be obvious the states of them are sort like a strawberry. Sketch out the middle, and afterward move along people.

Step 13: All that is truly left to do is draw in the greater part of the leaves, and after that a percentage of the stems. Sketch in the rib lines that characterize every leaf. Eradicate the aides and missteps that you attracted step one to tidy up the drawing.

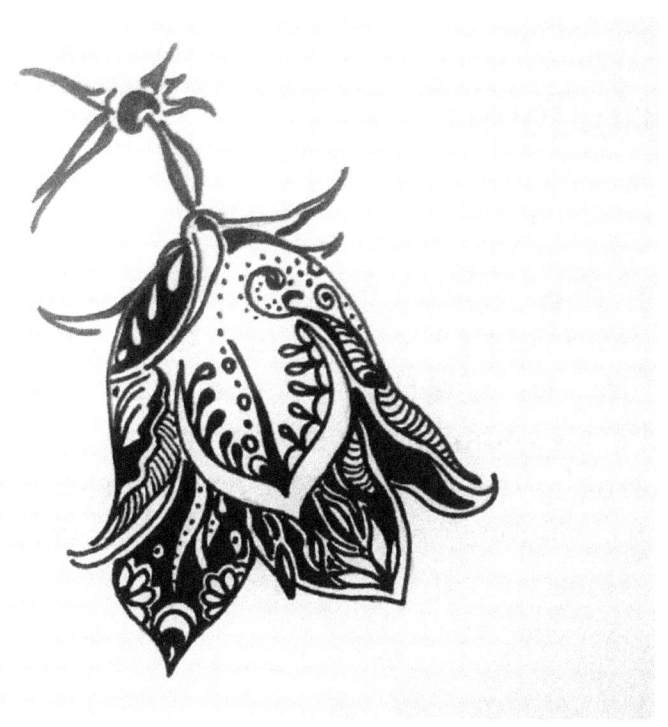

Step 14: Since you have got done with drawing out these flowers, you can have a great time coloring them in. This was great fun would it say it wasn't?

Conclusion

So you need to learn how to draw. Drawing, whether reasonable pictures or fun kid's shows and Japanese manga, all begins with the nuts and bolts. Every sort of drawing has its own particular peculiarities and livens so you will need to set aside some an opportunity to concentrate every classification except at the earliest reference point you need to concentrate on these basic tips to kick you off.

Get the Right Drawing Materials: Pencil and Paper

Regardless of what you do, you'll need to begin with the right arrangement of pencils and paper. Begin with the right kind of paper. Dodge sheets that are lustrous in light of the fact that they can be excessively smooth, keeping the surface from getting the rock of the pencil's lead. Try not to go for old paper either in light of the fact that they get excessively. Office paper and printing paper are a percentage of the best.

Concerning pencils, this can be confounded relying upon your inclinations however there is a standard that most artists stick with. For your beginning sketches and blueprints you'll need weak lines and a hard pencil is best for that. Go for a HB pencil for those introductory frameworks. When you need to begin including darker lines and shades then move to delicate evaluation pencils. Most artists utilize 2B, 4B, and 6B evaluation pencils for darker lines and shading.

Begin by Drawing Basic Shapes

Professional artists can draw shapes and lines right out of their head yet for an amateur you will need to begin with a format. The most ideal approach to make your own particular format is to ace the essential shapes. By mastering how to draw an elliptical or egg you can learn to draw a human face. By mastering how to draw squares, rectangles, and calculated lines you can draw the layout to draw immense robots and war machines.

The primary spot to begin is the egg shape. Expert this alongside oblongs and circles. Use them to draw faces. This will offer you some assistance with studying the best possible extent of the human face and later the human body. By mastering this you can utilize essential shapes to draw a human figure in any posture.

www.ingramcontent.com/pod-product-compliance
Lightning Source LLC
Chambersburg PA
CBHW080711190526
45169CB00006B/2327